To me, life feels like a race with no view of the finish line. Every turn seems to bring a new obstacle, and sometimes I feel unprepared to conquer it. With this life comes no training, no manual. I don't hear the voices cheering me on; I feel like I am running this all alone. Life is not a fairy tale. We think we can predict the next event, but most times we are wrong. Sometimes I feel like I am running in circles. I've seen this obstacle before. It seems, when I take another route in the race, to avoid the mountains I don't feel strong enough to climb, I only find them again in the pathways I thought were safe. Sometimes I feel like giving up. Sometimes I feel like it would be easier to let go of GOD and live my life in sin. I feel like maybe Satan would not bother me so much. Maybe the obstacles would move. But then, I imagine heaven!

Taken from Day 23: Then, I imagine Heaven!

40 Days with my Father

Insights from a 40-Day Fast

Katrina M. Nixon

40 Days with my Father

Insights from a
40-Day Fast

Katrina M. Nixon

Healthy Life Press
Arvada, Colorado

40 Days with my Father
Copyright © 2017 by Katrina M. Nixon

Published by:
Healthy Life Press • Arvada, CO 80003
www.healthylifepress.com

Author: Katrina M. Nixon
Designer: Judy Johnson

Printed in the United States of America

No part of this publication may be reproduced, stored in a retrieval system, or transmitted in any form or by any means—for example, electronic, photocopy, recording—without the prior written permission of the author, except for brief quotations in printed reviews.

Library of Congress Cataloging-in-Publication Data
Nixon, Katrina M.
40 Days with my Father

ISBN **978-1-534978-48-5**
1. Christian Life / Prayer; 2. Christian Life / Spiritual Growth

Unless otherwise identified, Scripture quotations are from the HOLY BIBLE, King James Version. This Bible version is in the public domain.

Capitalizations that do not conform to the *Zondervan Christian Writer's Manual of Style* are the author's choice, for emphasis.

Disclaimer: The opinions expressed in this book are those of the author, and may or may not represent the official views of Healthy Life Press, its Publisher, or any of its other authors.

Most Healthy life Press resources are available wherever books are sold. Distribution is primarily through *Amazon.com*, *deepershopping.com*, and *healthylifepress.com*. Multiple copy discounts available directly from Healthy Life Press. Wholesale distribution is through *springarbor.com* (a division of *IngramContent.com*), and *deepershopping.com*. Our ePublications are available through *healthylifepress.com*, *Amazon.com* (Kindle), *BN.com* (Nook), and for all eBook readers through *deepershopping.com*. Wholesale pricing is available through *IngramContent.com* (*springarbor.com*).

Do not begin a fast of significant length without discussing your plan with your personal physician, who should be able to provide guidance regarding how or whether you should proceed.

Contents

Thank You		ix
Dedication		xi
Introduction		xii
Day 1:	GOD dropped me in HELL!	2
Day 2:	The Border Collie	8
Day 3:	Perseverance!	14
Day 4:	LORD, please grant me tolerance.	20
Day 5:	Did you crucify my SAVIOR?	26
Day 6:	GOD, please teach me to forgive, AGAIN!	30
Day 7:	Do you really believe in GOD?	36
Day 8:	The Good Wine in Hell!	42
Day 9:	LORD, LOCK IT UP!	46
Day 10:	Damaged, but not destroyed!	52
Day 11:	Shackles of guilt!	58
Day 12:	The right thing at the wrong time.	64
Day 13:	Use me, LORD!	70
Day 14:	The Call of GOD!	76
Day 15:	The Message matters!	82
Day 16:	Your past is irrelevant to GOD!	88
Day 17:	GOD gave me goosebumps.	92
Day 18:	"Eli, Eli, lama Sabachthani?"	98
Day 19:	If you think GOD isn't listening . . .	102
Day 20:	Blessed to bless!	106
Day 21:	You've got a fan in Heaven!	112
Day 22:	Be specific when you pray!	116
Day 23:	Then, I imagine Heaven!	122

Day 24: I saw an angel!	126
Day 25: Winner gets your soul!	130
Day 26: The curse of riches!	136
Day 27: GOD gave me peace!	142
Day 28: GOD's favor!	148
Day 29: LORD, post a guard at the gate of my lips	154
Day 30: Troubling waters!	160
Day 31: Never leave a man behind!	166
Day 32: "Vengeance is MINE," saith the LORD!	172
Day 33: Is your life Gospel worthy?	178
Day 34: GOD's silence.	184
Day 35: LORD, please enlarge my territory!	188
Day 36: You don't know love, like GOD knows love.	194
Day 37: Where GOD works, Satan plays!	200
Day 38: Know your enemy!	210
Day 39: A vision of the second coming!	214
Day 40: My help cometh from the LORD!	218
About the Author: The Katrina Highway	224
Conclusion	232
Resources from Healthy Life Press	236

Thank You

Thank YOU, GOD, for all that YOU have done. For loving me in spite of what the world thought of me. For being there for me when I was not there for myself. For using me, when I thought there was nothing left of me to use. For the fire YOU have dragged me through, fulfilling purpose in my life, I am grateful. Although it pained me greatly and at times I felt defeated, now I understand and I am grateful. I love YOU, with all of me.

Over the 41 years of my life, I've met so many wonderful and interesting people. Some of you have served your purpose and moved on, while others have stayed, serving a new purpose daily. I am grateful for this journey, grateful to everyone I've met on the way, every lesson learned and every mountain you've helped me to overcome. I am even grateful for those who have placed mountains in my path. Without them, I would have never learned to climb, nor experienced the joy of overcoming.

To all of my sisters and brothers given by CHRIST, forever I will stand with you, side by side, fighting the battle for our salvation. Thank you all for the advice you have given, the prayers, the hope, the love, even the difficult moments that helped to strengthen and bring me maturity, for everything. Thank you to all the instrumental people who have passed through my life helping, inspiring, challenging and/or encouraging me, especially my guardian angel Mr. Ednal Collie & Bahamas Academy, Gregory Miller, Anita Collie, my blood and spiritual family. The seeds you have planted in my life have blossomed when you weren't looking. Your patience and prayers over my life made the difference. May GOD's purpose be fulfilled in your lives. I love you. Do not give up on GOD.

To everyone who has passed through my life, leaving me hurt, angry, depressed, and rejected, thank you. Without the pain you poured into my life, I may never have found my way to the arms of my FATHER, the only arms that have ever embraced the pain away.

Thank you Healthy Life Press for taking a chance on a first-time author. I pray for a blessed partnership.

To everyone who has opened this book, I pray for a genuine love and closeness to GOD, one that will draw you to know truths and never compromise in your service to HIM. For all those who have felt abandoned by the FATHER, at least once in your life, those who have cried out and no answer returned, those who have had countless moments, feeling what seemed like the absence of GOD, this book was written just for you. Be encouraged.

Dedication

To my High School Buddy,
Sacha Miller-Johnson,
who one day said,
"These devotionals of yours will all fit nicely in a book."
For allowing the FATHER to use you to inspire me,
this one's for you.

Introduction

Is GOD real? In the silence of my heartbreaking nights, I've felt the winds of GOD. In the disappointments of my worthless life, I've seen the evidence of GOD. In my most painful moments when I stood rejected, I've been comforted by the embrace of GOD. In my times of despair, I've held the hand of GOD, and HE has carried me over the thresholds of anguish. GOD, in all HIS greatness, has made provisions to wipe away the tears from the face of this filthy, insignificant, ungrateful sinner.

When my heart burned with desires, desires of just comfort, I prayed. When the world seemed to pass me by, step over me, forget me and cast me aside, I prayed. In my secret place, in the depths of my tormented soul, I've whispered prayers, in my mind, which no one can hear, and GOD, GOD answered me. When all hope seemed lost, and I thought the ground would open to receive me, I prayed, and GOD answered me.

I don't talk about GOD because I want to believe. I talk about GOD, because *I do believe*. GOD has shown me that HE is, HE has been, and HE will be, eternal.

I wish you could see what I've seen. I wish you could experience the things I've come through, knowing that only GOD could have rescued me. I wish I could make everyone understand that GOD is real, and HE listens. I wish I could make you see.

The FATHER is eternal. HE is merciful, patient, and forgiving. My words are not enough to describe the greatness of GOD. Know that HE is not a creation in the minds of idle historians. There is truly a GOD.

During my annual 40-Day Fasts, June 4th – July 13th in both 2014 and 2015, I laid my flawed character before my SAVIOR. I gave

HIM the broken pieces of my life. The pages that follow are the words that came out of me as HE began to mend me. I pray that what I share is not in vain, but serves a purpose in the lives of all who have chosen to read. I pray that I can help you to understand that GOD is truly present and active, as HE has always been. The events in my life have testified to HIS existence.

Day 1

"O LORD GOD of my salvation, I have cried day and night before THEE: Let my prayer come before THEE: incline THINE ear unto my cry; for my soul is full of troubles: and my life draweth nigh unto the grave.
I am counted with them that go down into the pit: I am as a man that hath no strength: Free among the dead, like the slain that lie in the grave, whom THOU rememberest no more: and they are cut off from THY hand. THOU hast laid me in the lowest pit, in darkness, in the deeps. THY wrath lieth hard upon me, and THOU hast afflicted me with all THY waves. Selah."

Psalm 88: 1-7

GOD dropped me in HELL!

When I thought my troubles were becoming too much to bear, I dropped to my knees and prayed. I asked the LORD to help me. I told HIM I just couldn't take it anymore. GOD picked me up and carried me to a place I had never known. I passed horrifying things on the way, but took comfort in knowing that I was safe in the arms of GOD, and no harm would ever come to me. HE took me to a dark and cold place, I didn't understand. HE lifted me higher. I felt GOD was showing me that HE will carry me, always. Then, HE held me over the awful abyss of Hell. HE looked me in my eyes. HE cried. I was confused. Then, HE dropped me. GOD dropped me into the torments of Hell!

I sat in Hell for longer than I could remember. I cried, I complained, I got angry, confused, I waited. I prayed, "GOD, why have YOU forsaken me?" I looked up from the place where my soul withered inside me, a place where peace would never reside. I saw GOD, still there, the pain on HIS face I didn't understand. Why didn't HE just pick me up? I have suffered long enough. When will GOD pull me out of this agony? I asked HIM every day, "LORD, what have I done to deserve this?" HE just looked on, not a word.

But the pity on HIS face was enough to tell me HE cared, although HE didn't try to save me. Years went by. Every day I looked up, GOD was still there. Though my suffering increased, HE never tried to save me. But HE watched, every day. HE listened every time I prayed. HE was there every time I needed to see HIS face, but why didn't HE save me?

The day came when the fire burning around me ignited a fire in me, and I took to the walls of Hell. I started to climb. Every time I got a little ways, I would fall and just sit there, and cry and pray, looking up at GOD. I thought if HE saw me trying to get out, HE would understand that I really wanted out, and HE would save me. But HE didn't. HE didn't save me. It drove me, because I wanted so badly to get back up to the place where GOD was, the place I thought was the worst of it, before HE dropped me to where I would know that it was not as awful as I thought it was, before it was as awful as it is now. I climbed again, this time, I looked up at the face of GOD, and I saw HIM smiling. Then I fell. I felt that GOD smiled because HE knew I wouldn't make it out. Confused, I figured that GOD did not love me, HE wanted me to stay in this torment. But every time I fell, HIS smile would leave HIS face. Every time I climbed, HIS smile would return.

Something about that smile on the face of GOD gave me new motivation, and I climbed again, this time, I kept my eyes on GOD. I made it out of the mouth of Hell. I realized that as long as I stayed focused on GOD, the torment, the obstacles, the burdens, the journey out of Hell seemed so much easier.

At the top, GOD wrapped HIS arms around me and I felt HIS tears beating, like rain, on my shoulders. I asked HIM, "FATHER, why didn't YOU help me?"

HE said, "Katrina, this life that you must live, will never tire of obstacles. The journey ahead of you will never get easier. You will find yourself all alone, with no one to give you a hand. You will go without the things that you feel are important. You will cry for help and no one will answer. I need you to be strong, to know that I am with you. I need you not to give up when the road seems like an endless torture, because I am with you. I am not here to move the obstacles out of your way. I am here to give you strength to beat the odds. Don't let Satan see you defeated, ever. Down in that pit, I saw Satan behind you. Every time you fell, he smiled, when you climbed, his smile left his face. Had I helped you out, as Satan knows I can, the pain on his face would not have been as great as it was, when he watched you, like a true Soldier in CHRIST, pull yourself up out of that pit. I waited here, and didn't move, because I love you, I am pulling for you and I want to be able to say, I am so proud of you. Make no mistake, Katrina. Although I didn't reach down MY hands and pull you up, I am still the fight in you."

It is a greater victory for the Kingdom, when we become so strong in CHRIST that we do not give up despite the odds against us. It is agony for Satan to watch those of us, who were once weak, become so strong, so determined, that we rise. No matter how many times life knocks us down, we rise. Satan expects that we would fall; it doesn't amuse him. He expects that GOD will help us; it doesn't amaze him. The Devil does not expect that we would take on the very same obstacles, with greater strength every time, and finally, become victorious. We must be strong in our walk with CHRIST, expecting trials, and prepared to fight for our souls. GOD has not forgotten us. HE does not expect us to fail. GOD wants us to fight, to be strong and determined in our Christian walk. For this reason, HE will watch, and push, and hope for us to climb out of the pits that we wish HE would simply pull us out of.

Sometimes I look back at my old photos and remember how I thought I was so fat and ugly then, but when I got older and had put on more weight, I realized that what I thought was bad, really wasn't, just like some situations I experienced, which I thought were the worst ever, until things got even worse. Can you think of something you went through that you thought was the worst thing a person could ever experience? How do your feelings about that situation differ now from how you felt about it going through it? Also, is there something that keeps beating you that you are constantly faced with? How can you work toward conquering that obstacle so it does not affect you so terribly?

_____

_____

_____

_____

_____

_____

_____

_____

Day 2

"I am the GOOD SHEPHERD,
and know MY sheep,
and am known of MINE.
As the FATHER knoweth ME,
even so know I the FATHER:
and I lay down MY life for the sheep.
And other sheep I have, which are not
of this fold: them also I must bring,
and they shall hear MY voice;
and there shall be one fold,
and one shepherd."

John 10:14-16

The Border Collie

I have found myself in some situations where I have questioned GOD. I felt abandoned, like I was on my own. Sometimes things got so bad I felt that GOD, for some unknown reason, was raining HIS wrath on me. I could not understand what was going on, where I was headed and why everything was going so wrong. Situations can get so bad, so deep, so trying. It felt like I was physically pushing my way through a maze, hitting dead ends at every turn. It was very frustrating.

If you have ever been on a sheep farm or watched a movie featuring one, you may very well understand what I am about to tell you.

I have heard it said that a "Border Collie," a dog breed, is born with that natural instinct to herd sheep in their rightful place. This is how it works. Every day the Shepherd lets his flock out to graze. When it is time to gather the flock back into their pen, the Shepherd uses his dog to round up the sheep. The dog runs back and forth around the sheep, barking and showing great aggression. The sheep move in the opposite direction to get away from the dog; this is the plan. This is the way the dog forces the sheep back into the safety of their pen. The Shepherd knows this is the plan and so does the dog, but the sheep really do not understand. Otherwise, they would run straight for their pen to avoid the dog.

Imagine how frustrated the sheep must be. One minute they are eating grass, undisturbed, then, the next minute, it seems like an attack for no apparent reason. It must be very confusing not knowing why that animal is barking so fiercely and coming at them from every angle. They simply do not speak the same language. If they could, I imagine the entire process would become much easier. I am sure the dog would love to save his time and energy and just tell the flock to get in their pen. But when such communication is not an option, the alternative methods could seem harsh, if you do not understand. Honestly, the dog's first motivation is not the sheep. He is trying to please his Master. He knows that his Master, the Shepherd, will not rest until every single one of his sheep is safely in the pen. The Dog knows that if he gets all of the sheep in that pen, it will greatly please his Master. That farm dog lives his life for the moment he has successfully brought joy to his Master, by securing the prized possession. You see, the dog is only the hero because he secures the true prize, the sheep.

Although the sheep do not understand all of this, all that barking is for their well-being. What seems like an attack is a force driving them in the right and safe direction. The sheep may be blind to the fact that there are wolves lurking, hoping for that fat feast, but the Shepherd knows, and that is enough for him to want to keep them secure.

A lot of times we do not understand why life is going the way it is. We do not understand why we are not in control of our situation. There comes a time when we have to realize that the time to graze is over and it is time to come to safety. Reality is not like the movies where you always see the danger that has been avoided. In life, in reality, you may never see what GOD has chosen to rescue you from. HE knows what is right for you and where you need to be in order to keep you safe from the wolf. Even when you do not understand, GOD loves you enough to find a way to communicate with you, although, at times, it may seem harsh.

Sometimes we give Satan too much credit. We blame him for all the pain in our life, when it could very well be GOD pushing us into our purpose. I don't always like the direction my life goes in, but, I have found at least one situation where a harsh distraction led to my best interest. Maybe GOD has saved me from other things that I don't even know about. I know HE watches and protects me, because every so often, HE sends a "Border Collie" to force me into the safety of my pen.

As we learn to put our trust in HIM, we will become less confused about the barking. We will come to realize that even though we don't understand, the intentions, the final outcome, is for our best interest. We will learn to be grateful for those moments when GOD's "Border Collie," the "HOLY SPIRIT," begins to push us in another direction, knowing that GOD must be saving us from harm, or ushering us to some place safe, some place better.

The first time I lived in Freeport, Grand Bahama, I was so blessed. I didn't hesitate to move back there, but things were different. Things got so bad that I had no choice but to move. I cried on the flight from Freeport to Abaco. I couldn't understand why GOD didn't come through for me. But once I made it to Abaco, my entire life changed. I got a job right away and lived pretty well. I didn't see it then, I didn't understand it, but now I do. Can you relate? Can you think about a situation where you had to come out of your comfort zone into a place you did not want to be in, and found it worked out best for you? Are you faced with a similar situation now? Are you finding that you have to make a decision you would rather not make? Is it possibly that it may actually work in your favor?

_____

_____

_____

_____

_____

_____

_____

Day 3

"Therefore being justified by faith, we have peace
with GOD through our LORD JESUS CHRIST:
By WHOM also we have access by faith into this
grace wherein we stand, and rejoice in hope of the
glory of GOD. And not only so, but we glory in
tribulations also: knowing that tribulation worketh
patience; and patience, experience; and experience, hope:
And hope maketh not ashamed; because the
love of GOD is shed abroad in our hearts by the
HOLY GHOST which is given unto us."

Romans 5:1-5

Perseverance!

Way back in 2002, a coworker and I had parked on the beach to enjoy our lunch. We both each had a nice ribs dinner, and the restaurant must have been feeling pretty generous because I have never had that much meat on a plate.

In the distance we saw a dog approaching. I don't know how far he came from, but from the point we saw him to where we were, was quite the journey for a weak animal. He looked tired and hungry, staggering from side to side, sniffing the ground and looking around, careful not to be hit by the passing cars. He was the only dog around, and we thought: *What a feast he is about to have when he comes upon the many bones we were throwing in front of the car.* Dogs love bones; hungry dogs love anything. A lot of my bones went out there with meat on them, because it was so much food, I was just making sure I got the juiciest part of each rib.

As we continued watching him journey toward us, I became so happy for that little dog. I did not know when he had had his last meal, but I knew that soon he would have a tummy full. Then, just before he got close enough to smell what we were laying out there for him, he turned around and went back the other way.

Now I don't know if he did not like bones, or if he smelled a steak in the other direction. I don't know if he was just too afraid of people to come any closer. I do not know what made that dog turn around at that moment, but I know what it looked like to me. It looked like, right before he could get the buffet of his life, he gave up.

Maybe this was GOD using a real life event to give me wisdom. We never know what is just over that hill, unless we persevere. We will not know what GOD has laid out for us until we reach the place in our journey where HE intended us to be. The journey sometimes seems never ending, and the trials we fight along the way can appear to be a pointless battle we would seem no worst off if we just avoided. There are times we feel like giving up and giving in, because that which we wish to grasp is nowhere in our view. Even in our Christian walk, when we are plagued with trials, when we must endure those things and people who seek to destroy us, we wonder, why should we persist in doing what is right when GOD seems often absent?

"Because thou hast kept the word of MY patience, I also will keep thee from the hour of temptation, which shall come upon all the world, to try them that dwell upon the earth." (Revelation 3:10)

It seems I am always fighting something. Whether it is something internal, or someone external, my life is always a fight; quite an adventure, if I must say so myself. I have to give GOD thanks for making sure I am never completely bored. Life for me seems a constant struggle.

It is my opinion that struggles are GOD's way of drawing us closer to HIM. We should feel privileged when GOD gives us a reason to seek HIM. How do you convince someone who has everything, that he needs something, he needs GOD? It is better to need something in this life, to hope for something, to pray for something, to wish for something, to aspire toward a dream. We need to struggle. We need to suffer through something in this life. In our suffering we become stronger, wiser, and dependent on GOD. We learn from those trying experiences and become teachers to those who will suffer behind us. Suffering makes us humble, and a man who cannot humble himself cannot stand before GOD. The true measure of our strength becomes evident in how well we can persevere in times of suffering, times of struggles. How strong is your faith in GOD when you cannot see the blessing of the sun through the trials of the dark clouds?

I have met a couple of people who love to say, "Nothing bad can happen to me, because I am covered by the blood." I feel sorry for people with that mentality, because I don't know what will become of them when suffering does come their way. How will they stand in times of trials and tribulations? Will they lose faith in the blood that they thought covered and protected them from all harm and danger? Will their relationship with CHRIST become diluted by the obstacles in the path they expected to be clear and easy? Do they really believe that no harm can come to them? Are they then greater than JESUS CHRIST?

JESUS CHRIST was not only covered by the blood, HE is the blood. Yet, HIS entire time in the ministry of GOD was plagued with suffering. In the end, CHRIST was spat on, whipped, pierced, and crucified on a cross. CHRIST knew suffering, yet HE persevered. I cannot imagine how far the legacy of CHRIST would have come if HE had given up during HIS struggles. We may all have ended up lost sheep, without a Shepherd.

Your life, my life, may very well be in use by GOD, to win over someone else. The struggles we face may one day become a testimony to the faithfulness of our FATHER, if we persevere. Don't ever think you are greater than anything or anyone, good or bad, that this world has to offer. Be humble, expect obstacles, and pray for the strength to overcome them, to fulfill the purpose which GOD intends, to be used by HIM. Embrace suffering! It presents an opportunity to persevere, thus strengthening your walk and faith in CHRIST. In all things there is a purpose, but to see the glory you must not give up. You must persevere.

Day 4

"Behold, we count them happy which endure. Ye have heard of the patience of Job, and have seen the end of the LORD; that the LORD is very pitiful, and of tender mercy."

James 5:11

LORD, please grant me tolerance.

We would literally burn holes in our knees praying for GOD to move every obstacle that comes our way. Before HE can move the first one, another one surfaces. Obstacles are not to be moved, they are to be overcome! I have learned that if we fail at overcoming an obstacle, we will face it again. It may be a different place, and different people, but the same situation. We would become so discouraged at having to go through it over and over again. But it is GOD's love for us that keeps HIM lining us up with those obstacles. GOD needs us to be strong, enduring, and tolerant in our faith, because Satan spends our entire life sending problems our way. We cannot become cowards when it is time to fight the battle of our lives, the battle for our soul. I don't know how possible it is for a weak person to obtain rights to the Kingdom of Heaven. The road to heaven is very narrow, and it is paved with trials, tribulations, and obstacles at every bend. We must pray for tolerance.

For nine months I lived next door to a young lady who worked my nerves. Her back door was aligned with my bedroom. Every morning, every night, all day when she was at home, she would slam that back door. It would wake me up out of my sleep, disturb my favorite TV shows, and shake the very room. She didn't just slam this thing once. She would slam it three or four times, at a time. For nine months she did this. It would wrench a whole new nerve in the core of my soul. Oh, how I hated that. Sometimes I would slam on the wall in anger. I would be so angry. The only time that door didn't slam repeatedly, was when she was not home. For nine months that stupid door made my living very uncomfortable. I wished so hard one day that she would get her hand caught in that door while slamming it, or even better, her head!

Well one day, while I was on my annual 40-Day Fast, that door almost detoured me from salvation. I am guessing it was GOD who put it in me to pray, instead of slamming on the wall. Usually, I would pray that she would move or that I would find another apartment, but life has taught me that such would come with new obstacles of its own. This time, I prayed that GOD would make me more tolerant. Yes, I matured! I asked GOD if HE could help me to be able to tolerate the slamming of that door, so it would not bother me so much. I prayed that prayer and forgot all about it.

About two weeks after the prayer, around 12:00 in the afternoon, I noticed that half the day had passed, and the door had not slammed at all. I was not relieved, I was worried. My door-slamming neighbor lived alone with her young child. I knew she was home because the vehicle she was using was parked out front. In nine months, that door always slammed when she was home, at noon, it would have slammed about thirty times by now. I was tempted more and more to go next door and make sure she was okay. All kind of things went through my head. If something happened to her, what has become of the child? It's noon, has he eaten yet? Is he okay? Amazing. Well around 2:00 p.m., she walked out the front door with her son, and went on their journey. What a sigh of relief. Then it hit me, for the past two weeks, the slamming of that door had not bothered me at all. I was more bothered when it did not slam. GOD IS SO ABLE.

Sometimes, we just need to pray the right prayer. Tolerance is far greater than the movement of any obstacle. Tolerance is comprised of strength, growth, and maturity. Obstacles are there to meet us when we enter this world and they will be there to usher us out of this life. Avoiding them is an even greater obstacle within itself. Tolerance, to be able to stand in the face of adversity, is a gift, a gift GOD wants us all to have.

What is something that you really have no patience to deal with, an annoying neighbor, your boss, the barking dog across the street? Can you think of something that sets you off so strongly that you are more content to run away from it rather than to endure it? How would your life be easier if you were able to tolerate it? What is that annoyance causing you to miss out on? How can you now begin to enjoy life regardless of that thorn in the side of your happiness?

_____

_____

_____

_____

_____

_____

_____

_____

_____

Day 5

"But the chief priests and elders persuaded the multitude that they should ask Barabbas, and destroy JESUS. The governor answered and said unto them, 'Whether of the twain will ye that I release unto you?' They said, 'Barabbas.' Pilate saith unto them, 'What shall I do then with JESUS which is called CHRIST?' They all say unto him, 'Let HIM be crucified. And the governor said, 'Why, what evil hath HE done?' But they cried out the more, saying, 'Let him be crucified.' When Pilate saw that he could prevail nothing, but that rather a tumult was made, he took water, and washed his hands before the multitude, saying, 'I am innocent of the blood of this just PERSON: see ye to it.' Then answered all the people, and said, 'HIS blood be on us, and on our children.' Then released he Barabbas unto them: and when he had scourged JESUS, he delivered HIM to be crucified."

Matthew 27:20-26

Did you crucify my SAVIOR?

We all know that CHRIST was crucified on a cross, when all HE did was good. But did you know that it was people just like us who crucified CHRIST? CHRIST was not condemned by sinners, but by those who called themselves righteous, and refused to believe HE was who HE said HE was. CHRIST hung on a cross because people thought they knew all they needed to know about GOD, and felt that this MAN, called "JESUS" was out of HIS mind. CHRIST hung on a cross because people felt HE was blaspheming the name of GOD.

I am amazed as I sit back and really think about it. We claim to love and worship CHRIST, we celebrate and talk about HIS great sacrifice for us as HE hung on a cross, but we never stop to think long enough about what type of people put CHRIST up there on that cross. Be reminded, that Pilate, in all his power, did not sanction the crucifixion of CHRIST. He told the people that he saw no basis by which CHRIST should be crucified. The decision between JESUS CHRIST and Barabbas was given to the "people." People, just like us, had the power to save CHRIST from hanging on the cross, but they chose Barabbas, a criminal, and had CHRIST tormented, and hung on a cross, with a crown of thorns placed on HIS head. And as if that were not bad enough, they made a mockery of HIM, gambled for HIS clothes and pierced HIS side with a spear, all while HE was already dying. This terrible and unfair injustice, that we all mourn to this day, was committed by people just like us.

We think we would never take CHRIST's life this way, but that is because we already know who CHRIST is. Had we not known, we would very likely have done the same, thinking that we are defending GOD, when in fact, we are killing HIS only SON. We are just modern day crucifiers. We are the same people. We are the same people who believe we know what is right and will not hear anything else from anyone else. We are the same people who close our doors in the faces of those who come bringing the good news. We are the same people who turn their backs on those in need. We are the same people who use the house of GOD as a place that benefits us. We are the same hypocrites, preaching the gospel from our mouths, and loving Satan with our lifestyles. We are the same people who know the laws of GOD better than anyone else. We live by the law, but have no love in our hearts. We are the same people who make our mistakes behind closed doors, then criticize openly those whose errors are seen by others. We are the very same people who crucified CHRIST.

CHRIST did not have to die on a cross, even though the majority voted HIM to it. CHRIST had the power to walk on water, change water to wine, heal the lame, and raise the dead. Do you really think HE did not have enough power to stop HIS own crucifixion? HE did, but HIS crucifixion was allowed in order that the glory of GOD would be revealed. CHRIST died so that we could see our errors as people so likely to crucify CHRIST. We celebrate this crucifixion, but what have we learned? Nothing. We're the same people. We crucify CHRIST every single day.

We are those judgmental, racist people who refuse to accept

those who are either of a heritage we do not like, or, our very own, because we cannot see our own people being used by GOD. We walk around with the hammer and the nails every day. We crucified CHRIST. How can we claim to love GOD, to love CHRIST, and not love our very own? *"If a man say, 'I love GOD', and hateth his brother, he is a liar: for he that loveth not his brother whom he hath seen, how can he love GOD whom he hath not seen?" (1 John 4:20).* We are the same confused people, who think we know! But there is none so blind as he who will not see.

As we look around us, in our lives, in our surroundings, it is time to really see who we are. Are we the saints of GOD, or, are we the crucifiers of CHRIST? As this life quickly unravels, it is now that we need to identify our faults. Put down the hammer and the nails. Let us stand as the Christians who will NOT crucify CHRIST.

Day 6

*"For if ye forgive men their trespasses,
your heavenly FATHER will also forgive you:
But if ye forgive not men their trespasses,
neither will your FATHER forgive your trespasses."*

Matthew 6:14-15

GOD, please teach me to forgive, AGAIN!

Experiences like the following have taught me that GOD is, without a doubt, VERY REAL! Every time I bow my head and pray, I ask GOD for two things: to forgive my sins, and to help me become a better person. We forget that if we do not forgive each other, our FATHER will not forgive us. One day when I remembered that, I prayed in my mind that GOD would help me to forgive others, so that I can also be forgiven. GOD, in a week's time, brought three people right in my face, three people I had been holding eternal grudges against.

PERSON ONE: One of my school mates left the country and went elsewhere to continue his education. He wrote me often, the nicest letters, as a friend. I never knew he had other intentions. One time, he came to visit and stopped by to say hello. It was brief. After he left, he wrote me again, but made a mistake. He had been writing another one of our classmates, a male, and had gotten the letters mixed up. In this letter he was writing to my other classmate, he spoke about me in the worst way—things I am too ashamed to repeat. The letter had some sexual content in it. Up until reading it, I had no idea he felt that way about me, especially since we had never spoken in any other way, but as friends—never touched, never kissed. What made this situation even worse was that my mother opened my letter and read it. That was even more hurtful, because I never felt like the people closest to me thought much of me. This letter gave them confirmation that maybe they were right, and I was nothing much. I did not say anything to him about the switch up, until the devil fooled him one day to call. And, oh how I let him have it. That was over 20 years ago.

PERSON TWO: Even further back, when I was in the sixth grade, I had a music teacher that I really liked. One day she walked in the classroom and a group of us were talking, but, in the way of the world against Katrina, she singled me out, fussed me, insulted me, and embarrassed me in front of the entire class. I can still remember the feeling of the sweat draining down my armpits as she blew me away, telling me how I was fresh and forward and would be bringing a baby home to my mother by the time I was sixteen. You could have heard a pin drop in the classroom. All eyes were on me. Oh, what a day. I can still remember it like it was yesterday. I was about 10 at the time. I saw her again when I was 18. I walked right up to her and said, "I'm 18 now, and I haven't taken a baby home to my mother as yet." She smiled and I walked away. I saw her again when I was 24. I walked right up to her. With her smiling, I said, "I'm 24 now and I haven't taken a baby home to my mother as yet." When I was about 32 she sent me a friend's request on one of those social networks. I rejected it and sent her a note, "I'm 32 now and I haven't taken a baby home to my mother as yet."

PERSON THREE: I had spent seven years working in Customer Service in various banks. I was a pretty good teller—pretty quick, efficient, no differences. Then, one day, a $2,500.00 shortage popped up. I tore the place up looking for that problem. It had to be in the paper work; no one loses $2,500.00. We never found it. I ended up getting terminated. The teller before me had been terminated for a $3,000.00 shortage. We were careless, I guess. We couldn't blame anyone for leaving our drawers unlocked when we made short trips around the branch. After my termination, a little birdie told me the person after me had a $2,500.00 problem, and eventually, they found it in the possession of a young lady who was later terminated for a $10,000.00 theft from treasury. She had been suspected for a while and for all of this missing cash, but, they could not prove it, and they didn't try. She sat next to the very cubicle where everyone's cash came up missing. Which bank has cameras that are not focused on the draw and customer of each teller? It's just that Katrina luck. This was over 12 years ago.

Here it is, I am praying to GOD to teach me to forgive, and, within one week from the prayer, I get "Friend Requests" from these three people whom I have not heard from for many years. And, I sure did let it out on the first two. I let them have it. Person 3, I just rejected. Both person 1 and person 2 responded almost identically, asking me to forgive the errors of their youth. I did not handle that correctly, not for someone asking GOD to help them to forgive. I hold no guilt for how I originally dealt with it, because GOD knew that I had a problem forgiving, or I would not need to pray about it. I believe these events were GOD showing me how hard it is for me to forgive, and giving me a platform for change. A year later, person 3 surfaced again, and I accepted her "Friend Request." It was going fine, until . . .

She posted her wedding pictures on her personal page. It was a beautiful wedding, looked real nice and well paid for. Then, I sent her a note and said, "If an unrepentant thief like yourself, who has caused so many their jobs and reputations, can find such happiness, then there is hope for us all."

Why did I send that? It angered me to see someone, who had done so much wrong, experience happiness in life. Meanwhile, I, who would never intentionally cause harm to anyone, was sitting in the midst of struggles and unhappiness.

This, this is what we need to let go of. It is true that forgiveness is not for the other person. It is for us. Had I forgiven her and truly let that grudge out of my heart, I would not have experienced that anger. That anger is something only I felt and it only affected me. She is still happy and moving on with her life. The ability to forgive is a gift from GOD, because it sets us free. As I write this, there is still so much that I am holding in. I ask GOD how can I let go of this and act like it never happened, setting my abusers free? But GOD reminds me, as I am reminding you, letting it go does not free them, it frees us. Those who have offended us are not sitting in dead ends of their lives, they are moving on. Maybe they are even remorselessly hurting others. "Vengeance is mine," said the LORD, "I will repay."

GOD, please, teach me to forgive, AGAIN! This is my eternal prayer, that I should be so blessed to be able to truly forgive, and finally be freed from the unforgiveness that imprisons me. This prayer I pray for all those reading this. The ability to forgive and move on is a gift from GOD, the key to the shackles that chain our peace and happiness.

Day 7

"The fear of the LORD is the beginning of knowledge:
but fools despise wisdom and instruction."

Proverbs 1:7

Do you REALLY believe in GOD?

Some of us don't even know if we believe in GOD or not, because we have fallen into a routine. Some of us have been worshiping GOD so long that we have never thought to analyze our true perspective of GOD. If you have no fear of GOD, you really do not believe in GOD! A person who believes in GOD will always consider the appearance of their actions in the sight of GOD.

I have come to believe that not everyone who talks about GOD really believes in GOD. Not everyone who testifies about GOD truly believes in GOD. Not everyone who goes to church and knows a Scripture or two believes in GOD. Not everyone on the pulpit believes what they are teaching us. Some of us are just going with the flow of things. We have come to accept GOD as a part of life and a thing to do. Some of us do not believe that one day the heavens will open and our SAVIOR will return in the clouds. Some of us think GOD is just the ultimate debate, an opportunity to verbalize unnecessary intelligence. As the world quickly ravels to the end of its rope, NOW is the time to focus on your relationship with GOD and if you truly believe in HIM. NOW is the time to stop playing games with your salvation. NOW is the time to get it right. Do not be fooled into believing that you can be careless with your life on Earth and then get serious about GOD when you are enjoying the New Jerusalem. You have to get it right here first, in order to make it there. You cannot get to heaven doing on Earth what you cannot do in heaven.

It is not possible to believe in GOD, and not fear HIM. By fear, I do not mean to be terrified of GOD to the point that you are likely to jump off a bridge before you make a mistake. By fear, I mean to have such an understanding of GOD's Word and HIS will for your life, that your conscience is activated every time a desire to sin arises, knowing that GOD exists, that HE is watching you and, whether any earthly person knows your actions or not, you are guilty in the eyes of the LORD.

Consider this: if you go to church, sing your heart out, have an "Amen" for every word the Pastor says, are full of the spirit and even "speak in tongues," yet, you go home to a completely different lifestyle of sin, WITHOUT THE FEELING OF GUILT, you really don't believe in GOD. If you are content to take the word of others, without reading the Word of GOD for yourself, you really don't believe in GOD. How can you fear GOD, if you don't even know who HE is? When we enter into relationships or friendships, we take the time out to get to know the other person, realizing that only through knowing them can we please them. How can we have any relationship with GOD if we do not know HIM? GOD has given us a manual, it is called the Bible. You really need to read it from cover to cover at least once in your life. I am on my seventh time, and still finding things that I do not recollect from my previous times of reading it. Reading the Bible helps us to understand the GOD we serve. Don't let anyone tell you about GOD, as if you are not worthy of a personal relationship with HIM. Besides, the Bible is a very interesting book. There is more to it than Creation, the

Flood, Psalms, and Job. There are more interesting stories in the Bible than Daniel in the Lions' Den.

I once read a bumper sticker that said, "If you are living like there is no GOD, for your sake, I hope you are right." But, I know you are not right. There is a GOD, I have proven HIM. HE is not a game or a thing to do.

Have you ever met a person who is doing every wrong in the book, or committing an open sin, and tells you that if GOD came today they are going to heaven? I don't think they believe in GOD. Yes, no one knows when GOD and sinners reconcile, but, if you are sleeping comfortably with someone's husband when GOD comes, do you really think you will be caught up to meet HIM in the clouds? Either you have no understanding of GOD, or you don't believe in GOD. If GOD came today, with all that I try to do right, I know Hell is where I would be headed, because I am holding in too many grudges, and that is not going to work in Heaven. I don't want to go to Hell, I really don't want Hell to have a population, but we cannot keep saying we are going to heaven, if we are really not working toward it. This world has become too relaxed with Christianity. We are asking GOD to make provisions for our sins, but that is a whole other topic.

We all need to analyze our relationship with GOD and where we are truly headed. NOW is the accepted time. These are the end times. Are you ready? Or, do you believe there is nothing to get ready for?

The question here is very simple: Do you really believe in GOD? Are you mindful of your actions when no earthly person is looking? Do you feel the need to do that which is right even behind closed doors, knowing the ONE who holds your life is watching? Or, are you only good when there is a human audience?

Day 8

"I say unto you, that likewise joy shall be in heaven
over one sinner that repenteth, more than
over ninety and nine just persons,
which need no repentance."

Luke 15:7

The Good Wine in Hell!

I believe there is a celebration in Hell every time the righteous take a fall. The extent of our faithfulness to GOD determines just how big that celebration will be. At this point in my life, I may not be worth a can of soda. I long to be better; I am working toward better.

There are those of us who call ourselves Christians, but we are not trying to live right, we just put on a show for others. When we fall, they will not even call a meeting in Hell, because they have better things to do with their time. Our "Christianity" is not worth a glass of water in Hell.

There are those of us who have the LORD in our hearts, and every intention to do right, but we often make mistakes. We try our best to tell others about the Word of GOD, but within ourselves, we still battle. When we fall, and that guilt hits, it is that soda toast in Hell. It's not much to celebrate, because they expect failure from us. But they know we are trying, so they toast cans of soda to celebrate the fact that we are still weak.

There are those of us who live as rightfully as we can, GOD on the mind in every minute of the day, but we have those one or two sins that keep dragging us down. We fight it, but not as hard as we should. Sometimes we fall. We take it so hard when we do fall, that it takes us a bit to get back up. There is a bottle of wine in Hell waiting to toast to our mistakes, but it is not the good wine.

Oh yes, then there are those of us who live for CHRIST. We stay in the Word of GOD. We live by the Word of GOD, not as they have taught us, but as we have read for ourselves and prayed for the wisdom to understand. We are so heaven bound. Yes, we make mistakes but we get back up so quickly. Satan cannot make it to his wine cellar before we reconcile with GOD. There is the most expensive bottle of wine, sitting on a shelf down in Hell, that Satan looks at every day, hoping today may be the day he pops that cork. Every time we make a mistake, Satan smiles and heads for that bottle. We, knowing that GOD is faithful to forgive us, once we ask HIM, truly repentant in our hearts, we get back up and run straight back to the arms of GOD. Then Satan backs away from that bottle, so disappointed. That bottle sits on the shelf, waiting! Satan wants so desperately to pop open a bottle on behalf of our downfall. Stay in the arms of GOD. Let that bottle dust up on that shelf.

We should aspire to be worth the good wine in Hell! We should want our life in CHRIST to be so firm that Satan wants to celebrate our mistakes, but he will not get the chance. We should want GOD to sit on HIS throne, so proud and confident in us, that HE sends a message down to Hell on a regular basis, saying, "That bottle will not be leaving the shelf today." We should seek to be faithful. Faithful were Noah, Abraham, Daniel—their bottles of wine have been renamed for someone else, because Satan never got a chance to pop it on their behalf.

Do not settle for a soda toast in Hell, when you should be worth the good wine. I pray that we all aspire toward it. LORD, begin a new work in us that we should be found worthy of the best.

Day 9

"As for GOD, HIS way is perfect;
the word of the LORD is tried:
HE is a buckler to all them
that trust in HIM."

2 Samuel 22:31

LORD, LOCK IT UP!

Through GOD, and in time, we will come to realize that the things we fought so hard for were not worth all we have lost in the battle. I have so often asked GOD to take the things from me which are not in accordance with HIS will. I have learned to trust GOD and all of HIS decisions. I have learned, through suffering and my own disobedience, that if GOD has the final say, everything will be just fine.

When we decide to give GOD our lives and ask HIM to have HIS way with us, HE will, for all the right reasons, close some doors that we often journey through. There are some avenues in our lives we should not return to. However, GOD is not going to force you to do the right thing. The beautiful thing about GOD is that even though it leads to hurt for HIM, HE gives us free will to make our own decisions. That free will brings us a lot of grief. That free will keeps us re-opening the doors that GOD has closed for the safety of our very salvation.

We are so weak. This flesh that imprisons us, fails us more often than we are willing to admit. I know there are doors in my life that are better off closed, and I have seen my SAVIOR closing them again, and again, and again. HE knows that I will re-open those doors in the future, since HE knows all things. Yet, HE will still take HIS time, and close those doors every time I ask.

In the year 2001 I did my very first fast of thirty days, asking GOD to fix a situation that I had made a mess of. Two days before the end of my fast, in a dream, GOD said "No," and HE closed that door. I would not accept that; my flesh wanted what it wanted. For three years I kept re-opening that door that GOD kept closing, and for three years re-opening that door brought me nothing but pain, pain from self-inflicted wounds that GOD was faithful enough to nurse, every time. GOD helped me deal with the pain every time, knowing perfectly well that I would go back and re-open that door that HE kept closing. As time has faded, the wounds have healed, and I have come to realize why GOD kept closing that door. Through that situation and others like it, I have learned that those doors are better off closed when GOD shuts them. The flesh, however, is still weak, and will still try its hand at those closed doors. We fail to realize that GOD has our best interest at heart.

> *"'For I know the thoughts that I think toward you,' saith the LORD, 'thoughts of peace, and not of evil, to give you an expected end.'" (Jeremiah 29:11)*

Now, for the past year, I have found myself in a similar situation, re-opening those closed doors. How do you know when GOD has closed that door? When you find yourself strengthened enough to walk away from a situation which brings you only hurt and pain, then you know GOD is closing that door. Every time you go back to that situation, and find yourself in pain, you are opening that closed door. Sometimes, we feel that because something once brought us joy and happiness that it is eternal, and the thing for us, but this is not always the case. Some things are worth fighting for, but others are just seasonal, a lesson to be learned. Through GOD we can learn to tell the difference. Learn to enjoy the room when the door is opened, and walk away when the door is closed. Not everything or every one that comes into our life is permanent. When we fail to realize that, we get stuck in the past while the future passes us by.

I am praying, "GOD, not only do I want YOU to close those doors in my life, I give YOU the authority to LOCK IT UP! Don't let me re-open those doors, no matter how hard I try and how much I plead and knock until the blood drains from my knuckles, LORD, LOCK IT UP! YOUR will is perfect, YOUR plans are flawless. Not my will LORD, but YOURS be done. GOD, if YOU do not want it in my life, then neither do I! LORD, close that door and LOCK IT UP! YOUR will be done."

What is something in your life that you are struggling with? Can you think of something that you are praying for the strength to walk away from, yet, you keep returning to it? As you pray for the strength, write here the things you would love GOD to lock out of your life, so that you can move forward, and then think of ways in which you can avoid reopening that door, until HE puts the lock on it.

_____

_____

_____

_____

_____

_____

_____

_____

_____

_____

_____

Day 10

*"But we have this treasure in earthen vessels,
that the excellency of the power may be of GOD,
and not of us. We are troubled on every side,
yet not distressed; we are perplexed, but not in despair;
persecuted, but not forsaken; cast down, but not destroyed;
always bearing about in the body the dying of
the LORD JESUS, that the life also of JESUS
might be made manifest in our body."*

2 Corinthians 4:7-10

Damaged, but not destroyed!

My 1998 Dodge Neon was 14 years old by the time I purchased her. I had her for two years before she started to give me any real problems. It seemed that as soon as one thing went wrong, the entire car took a downward spiral. I was constantly putting water in her until they patched up that issue, then she would not start all together. The starter was replaced then she got going again. But she was not the same, not like she was before. Then one day, she broke down completely. No one I tried could tell me exactly what was wrong with her. Some guessed and their speculations cost me some money. In the end, she was laid up for a while.

A single female has no place dealing with a problem car. It was terribly frustrating. I finally sold her for $900 and moved on. Well, when I saw "Gloria" again, she was running perfectly and the new paint job they added had her looking like a brand new car. Just because I did not have the time or knowledge to invest in repairing her, did not mean that she was finished. There are cars that make it to the junk yard and end up completely destroyed, just because someone did not have the time or knowledge to repair the damages.

Gratefully, GOD never gives up on us, no matter how damaged we are. Sadly, failing to see our own value, we often give up on ourselves. We write ourselves off because of the little damages, when the fact that we are still standing makes it clear that we have not been destroyed. GOD is still willing to use us.

Regardless of what our journey in life was before we came to CHRIST, I believe that we all have a purpose predestined by GOD. Each and every one of us has been given a talent, a skill that is beneficial to the Kingdom of Heaven, to help us win this fight against Satan. As we come closer to the end of days, whether we are ready or not, we need to take up our swords and plunge straight into this war.

I also believe those of us who stand on the side of GOD should feel privileged to exist in such tragic times. For I believe that even before we have come to know ourselves, GOD knew us and chose us to stand at the front line of this war, when the battle rages its worst, where HE would confidently place HIS strongest soldiers.

I have taken up this cross because I truly believe in GOD. It is my prayer that my life, the suffering I have endured, the mistakes I have made, the tears I have cried, the failures that attempted to define me, and even the pain I never understood, would one day be a testimony to someone else. I pray that GOD uses me to do a mighty work for HIS Kingdom, for no greater privilege is there in living.

"Damaged, but not destroyed," has been a slogan of mine for many years. We need to realize that our wounds are not the end of us. As long as we are still standing, there is hope. We need to remember that GOD can use our brokenness. As a matter of fact, it is our brokenness that really sets a stage for GOD's greatness to be exposed. How can a person who does not know suffering tell me how to endure pain? If you have walked the road I am now traveling, then you can tell me how to best complete this journey.

GOD, through HIS infinite wisdom, has taught me to stop asking "Why" in times of despair. I have learned that my life and all of my experiences are lessons for both others and for me. I have learned to embrace the damages in my life and my character. Because I am still standing, I have not been destroyed. With all of my damages, I can still be used. People can be cruel and would love to remind you of your past and your faults. It is nothing but Satan trying to detour you, silence you, and break you down. If everyone who made mistakes in their life or possessed imperfections became an outcast from GOD, HE would have no one to use.

Everything, right or wrong, that you have endured in this life, can be used as a testimony to someone else. We must learn to be stronger and to channel our errors and what seems like damages in our past, in the right direction. GOD can use you.

I remind you, the deeper you have traveled down that destructive pit, the brighter the light of GOD shines in your life, when others realize how far up you have had to climb. So if it did not kill you, let it make you stronger. Embrace the damages you have lived to talk about. They may have hurt you, but they did not destroy you.

Have you ever given something away or sold something that you thought was worthless, then found that the new owners restored it to life? Take a moment to reflect on you. Is there something about your life and/or your past that you feel makes you useless or unworthy? Use these lines to focus on the good in you, think about all the beautiful things you can do. How can GOD use you now, despite who you once were? What are you prepared to do, to share for the Kingdom? How can your life, your past, your scars be a testimony to someone who has not yet found the strength to overcome?

_____

_____

_____

_____

_____

_____

_____

_____

_____

Day 11

"For all have sinned, and come short of the glory of GOD; being justified freely by HIS grace through the redemption that is in CHRIST JESUS: whom GOD hath set forth to be a propitiation through faith in HIS blood, to declare HIS righteousness for the remission of sins that are past, through the forbearance of GOD; to declare, I say, at this time HIS righteousness: that HE might be just, and the justifier of him which believeth in JESUS."

Romans 3:23-26

Shackles of guilt!

Back when I was eleven or so, there was a case of baby juice purchased for my baby brother. I sneaked a taste of one and loved it. I did not want my Mother to know that I had been in the juice, so I filled the empty space with water and closed it back. Then, I got addicted and must have done it with the entire case of juice. Well when my Mother realized what had happened, she was highly upset. She wanted to know who did it. I said it was not me. My seven-year-old brother ended up taking the fall for it and I will never forget the beating he got that day. It seemed to have lasted for hours.

For 27 years I held the guilt of that in. I told myself I was just a child, let it go. I told myself I did not say he did it. I just said it was not me. For years, many years, every time I would get happy about something, remembering the lie I told that caused my innocent little brother such a punishment would end my joy. For years I held it in. Every time it came up, I asked GOD to forgive me and promised HIM that one day I would confess. For 27 years the LORD allowed that to beat on my conscience.

During my fast, as I was going over all the pain people have caused me and the lies they have told about me, the juice situation came back up. I told the LORD I would confess soon. This fear came over me and I could not stop trembling. It was like the LORD was saying, "NOW!" Trembling, like I was still 11 years old, I called my mother and told her that 27 years ago, my brother had taken a terrible beating for something I had done. Then I contacted my brother and told him how sorry I was and how it has haunted me all this time. I do not believe that GOD kept it on my conscience because HE was not willing to forgive what I did way back when I was a child. I believe that my brother was still hurting over it and GOD knew. The people we wrong just want to know that we are sorry and that we realize that we were wrong. I cannot begin to tell you what a relief it was to get that off my chest after 27 years.

However, we all have sinned and come short of the glory of GOD. We cannot let our faults, our sins imprison us. There is forgiveness in CHRIST. If we pay attention to man, we may easily forget this. We, human beings, are not as easy to forgive others, and there are times when the guilt of wronging someone can overwhelm us. I have been on both ends of unforgiveness. If we ask forgiveness of those we wrong and of the LORD, truly repentant, it is up to them to either forgive us, or hold that burden in their hearts. But know that GOD does not need approval from man to forgive. Do not allow others to make you feel unforgiven by the LORD.

Yours may not be a situation of wronging someone. You may have that one sin that often entices you and leaves you feeling like an outcast from GOD's grace. For me, it has been profanity. I swore like a drunken sailor. What really got me down about it was, I didn't miss and fire a word. I have that moment of reasoning that says, "Don't say it, Katrina. Don't swear." That is what really makes me feel bad about it, not that I swore, but that I ignored the voice that told me not to. Every time it happened, I took it like a train wreck. I thought, *Surely I am going to Hell now. GOD must be tired of me asking forgiveness for this use of profanity, that is why HE puts in my conscience not to do it.* I got depressed about it for at least twenty-four hours each time. I was not depressed because I swore. The depression was feeling like GOD was tired of me and those unnecessary words. The guilt of disappointing GOD made me feel like it was pointless to ask forgiveness, or even try to get back in GOD's good graces.

This very guilt that we carry sometimes leads us back down the wrong road. We feel like there is no hope for us, that GOD has washed HIS hands and turned HIS back on us. We feel like it is over, and there is no point in trying. That guilt that we feel is Satan using one of his best methods to keep us separate from the LORD. When we fall, we must learn to get back up and dust the guilt off! GOD knows our hearts and how we truly feel inside. GOD knows how it hurts when we make mistakes and how badly we want to do what is right. The good in our hearts is what is attractive to GOD, not what we wear, how we fix our faces, and what show we put on in the church.

Do not let guilt steal your soul. Be determined in your walk with CHRIST to get back up and move forward, trying a little harder each time to eliminate those mistakes, those poor habits from your character. I am certainly not saying do not be hard on yourself, for I believe when it comes to sin, we should be very hard on ourselves. Some people will make you feel like it is not so bad, but sin is never good. We should never accept it as a part of us. What I am saying is do not allow those sins to make you feel like an outcast from GOD. HE is faithful to forgive us when we ask, truly repentant, but we do need to work toward living without those sins as a part of our lives. We will fall; we are human. Those falls show us the flaws in our character.

Every stumble is a lesson that should strengthen you on your journey with CHRIST. Do not allow Satan to use your sins as shackles to imprison you. Although Satan manipulates us mentally into thinking they are still there, once forgiven by the FATHER, those shackles disappear.

Twenty-seven years is a long time to carry something on your chest. It dropped like bricks when I finally released it. Is there a burden you are carrying? Is there some mistake weighing so heavy on your chest that it has crippled your walk to happiness? What is preventing you from releasing it? Are there mistakes in your past which you have asked forgiveness for, but yet you still feel unforgiven? Write them here, pray once again for a final forgiveness, then next to them, write "Forgiven."

_____

_____

_____

_____

_____

_____

_____

_____

_____

_____

Day 12

"Wait on the LORD: be of good courage,
and HE shall strengthen thine heart:
wait, I say, on the LORD."

Psalm 27:14

The right thing at the wrong time.

An interesting and hurtful thing happened to me the day I wrote this devotional, it actually inspired me to write it. About a month prior, while moving some trash from the front of the yard, I found a tiny egg. I took it inside, because I love nature, and wanted to see what would come out of it. I kind of knew it was a lizard's egg. I made a swampy habitat for it in an old coffee container, but, I was told to keep it warm and that water seemed a bit too cool. Thinking I was doing the wrong thing, I took it out of that habitat and wrapped it in a napkin, figuring that would be warm enough. Well, someone said, if the egg is abandoned, what is inside is likely dead. Someone else said, give it a month, then open it, it is dead. So I marked on the calendar the very day I would crack that egg if it was not already cracked. I had been waiting for the day, feeling most certain the egg contained a dead lizard. The day came and I cracked the egg. It surely was a lizard. It seemed to still be developing fine. The liquid inside was still moist. After taking the lizard from it, and determining it was dead, I dropped it in the toilet. The thing started to jerk around. I took my tweezers and took it out of the toilet, and rested it on a sock, where I tried, and failed to save the lizard that my impatience had aborted. I felt just awful.

A couple months prior, I had decided to start growing trees, because I have a dream to have a farm. I went online and learned how to grow lemon and tangerine trees. I peeled the shell off the seeds and placed them on a wet napkin in a Ziploc bag. Every day I looked at them, knowing I could not grow anything. I didn't expect anything, but they started to develop just as I was told they would. I was also told that I waited too long to take them from the bag and put them in the ground. I put them in the ground anyway. After a couple weeks of seeing nothing new, I ripped them out of the pots. That is when I realized that those seeds had grown up to 4 inches of root into the ground. My impatience killed those trees.

This is who I am. The woman who wants things, prays for things, then puts my hand in it and mess it all up, because I go after the right thing, at the wrong time. Most times I feel like I will not get it anyway, so why not make a mess of it? Taking this perspective, it is possible to completely ruin your life. Reality is not a fairy tale. We are not guaranteed a happy ending no matter who we are and how hard we pray. We have to face life like everyone else. When we decide to give a situation to GOD, we have to allow HIM to be in charge. We have to take our hands out of it. Don't put a time limit on GOD. Everything happens in its rightful time, if we leave it to GOD, where we have placed it.

I believe, and have proven, that we can miss out on the opportunity of a lifetime, just by putting our hands in it at the wrong time. We love to say, "What's for me, I'm going to get." It sounds good, but, it isn't true. Because if you go and get what is for you, when it is not the time for you to have it, you can miss out on it for the rest of your life. You can destroy your blessing.

I don't have patience, and I'm afraid to ask GOD for it, knowing I need it. I have prayed for many things, mostly help with my character, but patience, I have been afraid to pray for. However, given the events leading to the death of my lizard and citrus trees, I think GOD has decided it is time for me to have that patience anyway, whether I ask or not. This is one of the many reasons why I love HIM so much. GOD will always make the right decisions for you, when you give HIM your life. I may not be praying for patience, but I am praying for some things that I am going to need patience to get.

I don't know, maybe I'm about to put my hand in something that I will make a mess of, because it is not the time. Maybe my little lizard experience is painful enough to teach me to wait. I did not learn it from the fruit trees. I will plant again.

Update: I am grateful to GOD for life's lessons. I am very grateful! A short time after writing this devotion, I was fortunate enough to find about a dozen lizard eggs. This time, I was patient. I even set up my camera from time to time to record the hatchings. I missed the first two hatchings but, amazingly caught the third one. I also have a lime tree growing nicely. I am very pleased that I learned my lesson on patience before my hands were put on abundance. I believe this is how GOD works. HE will give us our training on the smaller things, so that when we get the greater blessing, in the right time, we would not make a mess of it.

Today you may be praying for something that you have become very impatient about. Sometimes, the FATHER is saying, "Wait." It is not a "No," it just means it is not the time. It is not only the will of the FATHER we should respect, but also HIS timing. I see this in the couple that so loved each other that they rushed into marriage, but it didn't work. Then, as faith would have it, they remarried and lived happily ever after. Marriage was in their future, but not at that time. Can you think of something that you would like to have? Do you have everything you need to accommodate the blessing you are praying for? Are you mentally prepared for it? We think we want things, but sometimes we are just not ready. Are you ready for what you are praying for?

_____

_____

_____

_____

_____

_____

_____

Day 13

"So we, being many, are one body in CHRIST,
and every one members one of another.
Having then gifts differing according to the grace
that is given to us, whether prophecy, let us prophesy
according to the proportion of faith; or ministry,
let us wait on our ministering: or he that teacheth,
on teaching; or he that exhorteth, on exhortation:
he that giveth, let him do it with simplicity;
he that ruleth, with diligence; he that
sheweth mercy, with cheerfulness."

Romans 12:5-8

Use me, LORD!

Everyone has different gifts, and when you sit still and reason long enough, you will realize that your gifts are unique ways that GOD has used to communicate with and through you. I have been envious of people who have told me that GOD speaks to them, directly, like we talk to our friends. Why doesn't GOD talk to me? Being the sensitive soul that I am, I felt that maybe GOD does not care for me the way HE cares for others.

What a mess Satan must have our minds in, when we reach that conclusion, the idea that GOD does not love us as much as HE loves HIS other children. But, when I think about it long enough, I am so scary, if GOD spoke to me, I would very likely jump out of my skin and run out of the room before HE could get the next word out. We are different, made differently—different mentality and certainly different degrees of strength. Therefore, we have different gifts. Every gift is important and valuable. What is beautiful is, knowing that GOD has taken the time to custom-make HIS method of communication with you. How awesome is that? However, the truth is, those gifts are completely worthless if we don't use them for the purpose for which they have been given.

For my entire life, I can remember dreaming. I knew when I would see an old friend, when something was going to go wrong, when I would have a good day, when I would get the job I interviewed for, when I was going to quit. I have been shown, in my dreams, which roads not to travel. GOD has protected me more than I deserve. When I was just about ten, I had a dream that JESUS was on my porch. In front of HIM was a big, round, tin tub. It was filled with water and HE sent me out to bring people for HIM to baptize. At the age of ten, I knew what the dream meant. Thirty years later, I remember it like it was just last night.

They say that every time you help to bring someone to CHRIST, you get a star in your crown. My crown is empty. I have had so many opportunities to advertise my LORD, but I've been afraid. How can I tell the man I am sleeping with in sin, that GOD wants him? How can I tell the women I gossip with that it is time to change? How do I look someone I offended in the face and tell them that GOD is calling them?

It is fearful enough to think that GOD will come and find me still living in sin, but more fearful to think that I would have no credits to my name. To live an entire life on this Earth, to have traveled, to have met people, to have worked and been exposed to many environments, to spend time with a person and part ways, to see wrong, to do wrong, to know right from wrong, to live, to laugh, to enjoy life, and not have my life mean anything to GOD's Kingdom? What a waste.

With all of the distractions of this world, it is easy to forget what we are supposed to be doing here. We are workers for the Kingdom of GOD. Every person has a talent, a gift that money cannot buy, a gift that costs nothing to maintain, a gift from GOD for the benefit of HIS Kingdom, and what are we doing? We are taking our GOD-given talents and using them for Satan's gratification.

I pray that GOD will use me and show me the direction HE

wants my life to take. It hurts me to think that GOD may have given up on the call HE has shown me about my life, way back when I was just a child. I see children now standing at the pulpit, preaching the Word of GOD, and I feel ashamed. GOD is calling children to do what we, as adults, have failed to do. We should all be ashamed.

This is my prayer and this should be the prayer of all who seek to please the LORD: "Use me, LORD, to bring at least one home to YOU." Let us begin now, to pray that the FATHER would make clear HIS purpose for our lives, and give us the strength and courage to fearlessly follow the plan we are so privileged to have HIM outline for our lives. Let us die empty, using all that GOD has put in us to give to this world.

Like my gift of dreaming, I believe everyone has a way in which the FATHER guides them. Dreams, visions—some people just have a sixth sense, just a bad feeling about something ahead. You may not have noticed it before now, but here is the time for you to reflect on your inner strength. What is the unique design in your character which the FATHER may be using to lead you? How are you using that gift? How can you begin to use it more effectively and positively?

_____

_____

_____

_____

_____

_____

_____

_____

_____

_____

Day 14

"Behold, I stand at the door, and knock:
if any man hear MY voice, and open the door,
I will come in to him, and will sup
with him, and he with ME."

Revelation 3:20

The Call of GOD!

Can you remember the days before Caller ID? Some of us would attempt to disguise our voices to avoid certain calls. Then they gave us Caller Identification. The name on that screen, when the phone rings, determines how we will answer that phone, if we will answer it at all. They thought they got smart when they blocked their numbers, but we just don't answer those calls. Have you ever ignored a call you wish you had taken? Is it possible that you have ignored a call from GOD?

Some of us are intentionally ignoring that call. It is no accident that we don't take heed to the voice of GOD. We want more time to enjoy the sins we are not ready to walk away from and we expect that GOD should understand. We want GOD to wait on us. We will come to HIM when we are ready. Hasn't GOD been patient? Isn't it just gracious of our LORD and SAVIOR to sit patiently on the sidelines of our lives, waiting for the day we finally commit to HIM? What a marvel, this GOD who reigns.

> *"And ye have forgotten the exhortation which speaketh unto you as unto children, my son, despise not thou the chastening*

of the LORD, nor faint when thou art rebuked of HIM: For whom the LORD loveth HE chasteneth, and scourgeth every son whom HE receiveth. If ye endure chastening, GOD dealeth with you as with sons; for what son is he whom the father chasteneth not? But if ye be without chastisement, whereof all are partakers, then are ye bastards, and not sons. Furthermore we have had fathers of our flesh which corrected us, and we gave them reverence: shall we not much rather be in subjection unto the FATHER of spirits, and live? For they verily for a few days chastened us after their own pleasure; but HE for our profit, that we might be partakers of HIS holiness. Now no chastening for the present seemeth to be joyous, but grievous: nevertheless afterward it yieldeth the peaceable fruit of righteousness unto them which are exercised thereby." (Hebrews 12:5-11)

When GOD begins to call persistently, it is time to take heed. When your conscience begins to whip you daily, it is time to take heed. When you find the sins you enjoy are presenting themselves even more frequently than you would like, it is time to take heed. Even before you find all this occurring, it is time to take heed. Now is the time to answer the call of GOD. GOD calls us because not only does HE want to save our souls from eternal damnation, but HE has a purpose for our lives. GOD has a work for each of us to do. Some of us get so arrogant. We think that what we can offer the LORD is so awesome that HE will wait until we come into our calling. Our time may just be running out.

Every time I see a video circulating with a child preaching on the pulpit, it scares me. Seeing the youth, barely out of Pampers, coming in to the calling of GOD, has shown me that GOD does not need to wait on me or anyone else. GOD can use whomever HE chooses to do the work HE needs to have done. GOD's love for us keeps HIM waiting. There is nothing we can do, no talent that we possess that is so amazing and unique that GOD has to keep us here.

I want to encourage you to answer the call of GOD before the ringing stops. You do not want the day to come when HE no longer calls. We need the LORD a whole lot more than HE needs us. Don't believe that you must be perfect in order to come to the LORD. Come to the LORD as you are, and allow HIM to do HIS work in you. Be willing to submit to the call of GOD. That is what HE requires of us. I remind you that Saul was on his way to slaughter more of the Saints when the LORD called him. You may not be as blessed as Saul. Your stop on the road to destruction may be the last stop of your life. What if GOD plans to call just one more time? What if the last call, was the last call? I don't mean to terrify anyone, but the graveyards are filled with gifted people, some never having answered the call of GOD.

We all have a tugging in us from time to time. Every single person who has a belief in the FATHER has an activated conscience. Like the tugging I had to get this book written, I'm sure there is something you have been putting off. Write it here and say it out loud so the reality will set in that you know the FATHER has a calling on your life. Then, begin to work on it. Sometimes, it only takes a start. Or, you may have a bad habit that you are not quite ready to let go off. Today is the day to work toward moving forward; don't say "tomorrow." Write that bad habit here, next to it, write "Deleting," meaning you are removing it from your character.

_____

_____

_____

_____

_____

_____

_____

_____

Day 15

"And the LORD opened the mouth of the ass, and she said unto Balaam, 'What have I done unto thee, that thou hast smitten me these three times?' And Balaam said unto the ass, 'Because thou hast mocked me: I would there were a sword in mine hand, for now would I kill thee.' And the ass said unto Balaam, 'Am not I thine ass, upon which thou hast ridden ever since I was thine unto this day? Was I ever wont to do so unto thee?' And he said, 'Nay'.

Then the LORD opened the eyes of Balaam, and he saw the angel of the LORD standing in the way, and his sword drawn in his hand: and he bowed down his head, and fell flat on his face."

Numbers 22:28-31

See Numbers 22:22-34 for the story of Balaam and his donkey.

The Message matters!

We must be so careful who and what we focus on. We can be so easily manipulated and distracted if our focus is not on the right thing. I really don't like to hear the way some Christians go on about their Pastors or spiritual leaders. It is as if we worship them, and that should not be. I know people who will come near a heart attack just to hear their Pastor call their name from the pulpit. They would just brag about the way they seem to be a light in the eyes of their spiritual leader. "My Pastor likes this." "My Pastor told me this." "My Pastor." "My Pastor!" But what did you get from the word the Pastor preached in church? What is now your understanding of CHRIST? Are you going to church to help with forming a relationship with CHRIST, or, are you trying to be the Pastor's favorite?

Are you comfortable just attending Church, getting the Word and going home? Or, do you become discouraged when the Pastor uses everyone else and seems to overlook you? Do you feel honored doing what is right according to GOD, or, do you feel honored when the Pastor exalts you over the other members? Is your faith so strong in your Pastor that you are content to just believe whatever he or she says, without ever opening the Word of GOD for yourself? Who are you really trying to please? Are you afraid to do the wrong thing in front of your Pastor, yet would slaughter the very life of mankind behind the Pastor's back? I feel sorry for those who feel that way, because you have forgotten that GOD still watches all things, and that your Pastor or spiritual leader is just a vessel being used. You have also forgotten that your Pastor or spiritual leader is just a human being who is disposable, and you need to ensure that your foundation in CHRIST is strong enough to stand, even if and when your leaders fall.

On the other side of the coin, there are some of us who have a ministry inside that we refuse to use, because we know people are watching us behind the walls, and that our past is so muddy. If GOD used Saul, if GOD used a donkey, HE can use us. Don't let anyone discourage you from sharing the Word of GOD. The kingdom needs all the help it can get, because Satan has an army that none can number.

The point here is, we need to take our eyes off whoever is bringing us the Word. Some of us are so focused on the messenger, that we will only chose to believe the Word of GOD that comes from them, if we like or love who the messenger is. And that, my friends, is sad and unfortunate. You should measure the word being brought to you only by how well it lines up with what GOD has presented in the Bible.

Just as I want to say, do not focus on the person bringing the word, I also want to say, do not worry about who is more focused on you. If GOD has put a ministry in you, to share HIS Word, whether it is through song, teaching, preaching, poetry, dance, or whichever talent GOD has sewn into the fabric of your existence, do not be detoured. Do not let family, friends, enemies, your past sins, your short comings, anyone or anything, make you feel like you are not valuable to the Kingdom of GOD. It is always those closest to us, and even we ourselves, who make us feel inadequate.

CHRIST told HIS disciples: *Matthew 10:14-15, "And whosoever shall not receive you, nor hear your words, when ye depart out of that house or city, shake off the dust of your feet. Verily I say unto you, It shall be more tolerable for the land of Sodom and Gomorrha in the day of judgment, than for that city."* Continue to allow GOD to use you. HE will take your Ministry where HE wants it to be.

I will give you the perfect example. Back in 1995 I entered a speech competition. I had never been in such a competition before and don't know why my mouth quickly volunteered me for something my mind had given no thought to. First, I had to win in my church in order to compete with the winners from the other churches. Many times I thought of withdrawing, but GOD bless my High School Religion teacher who was also very active in my spiritual life. He told me not to give up. He saw something in me that I didn't see. Well, I won from my church and it was time to compete against the other churches. I was the last one to speak. In the competition were two ladies I had graduated from High School with. While they sat patiently through all the other speeches, when the moderator called my name, my old classmates got up and walked out. To them, I was not worth the time. But I got on that stage and did my best. There were times, during my speech, where the audience cheered so loudly that I couldn't hear myself. I felt too good to even worry about those who didn't find me worthy of their attention. I won that competition, missed a perfect score by four points.

At the end, a lady walked up to me, hugged me and said, "They should ordain you right now." The question of ordaining women had come up in our church right about that time. More than winning, it was beautiful that someone saw the work of GOD in me. It didn't matter that the only two people I knew in the competition had walked out on me; GOD's message went to those deserving. I didn't know them, but that made it better. They were able to identify the message without being tainted by their personal opinions of me. That day was so beautiful to me that I did not even remember how my old classmates walked out on me until 20 years later. I believe it was GOD who reminded me so that I can share it with you, for whatever reason HE feels it necessary.

Do not worry about those who do not respect your work for the kingdom; the loss is theirs. GOD will take you, use you, elevate you, and anoint you regardless of who refuses you. One thing I am certain of, the desire to share the greatness of GOD did not come from Satan. If they refuse to hear you, keep moving, you will reach your audience. After all, it is not how they view you, it is what they think of GOD. Satan is determined to silence the saints of GOD in whatever way he can. Do not give the enemy the glory of your testimony dying with you.

Additionally, I want to say to the spiritual leaders, that although we should not be so focused on your life, as humans, we are. Many of the spiritual leaders today are in the business for a paycheck. We are not mindful of our actions and our words until we are on the pulpits. Let us not forget, that although they should not be doing so, they are watching us. When we talk about GOD, then fail to practice what we preach, we lose credibility. Therefore, we should not go about our sins as if there is no one watching and as if it is acceptable. In this, we attempt to humiliate GOD. It does not matter who is watching. Some saints think there is no wrong in offending people who are not as saved as they would expect people to be. Some saints treat certain people with respect and love, while others they treat very poorly. We are only as good as we treat the person we think the least of. A good tree cannot bear bad fruit, so if there are corrupted fruits hanging from your tree, then, you are not the good tree you would have some to believe.

For those of us who talk about GOD, yet live openly like there is no GOD, HE will, in a very unpleasant way, expose us for who we are. GOD will not allow HIS sheep to be led astray by careless Shepherds. If you are not a true believer in my FATHER, now is the time to consider a new line of work. Resign, before you are terminated.

How do you feel about your spiritual leaders? Do you think that it is possible that their failures may affect you deeply? Or, are you a leader? We are all setting examples. What are some of the things you think you should eliminate from your character in order to show yourself to be more CHRIST-like?

_____

_____

_____

_____

_____

_____

_____

_____

_____

_____

Day 16

"When JESUS had lifted up HIMSELF, and saw none but the woman, HE said unto her, 'Woman, where are those thine accusers? Hath no man condemned thee?' She said, 'No man, LORD.' And JESUS said unto her, 'Neither do I condemn thee: go, and sin no more.'"

John 8:10-11

See John 8:1-11 for the story of the woman caught in adultery.

Your past is irrelevant to GOD!

Satan has some very creative ways of holding us prisoner to our past. It's like the bank, the interest keeps growing until one day, the principle is paid off, and you are still paying on the interest. We make mistakes, we ask forgiveness, yet we still find it hard to move on, because the guilt has got a hold on us.

We cannot imagine the mercies of GOD. GOD does not care about what we have done in our past, or what disaster our life has evolved from. GOD sees the excellence in us and our desire to serve HIM, both of which can be used for HIS glory.

I always reflect back on the story of Jacob. Jacob, from birth, seemed such a scandalous person. Jacob, when his father Isaac was very old, at his mother's advice, deceived his father into believing that he was his brother Esau, which led his father to give him (Jacob), Esau's blessing as the first born. Esau then sought to kill Jacob. Jacob's mother sent him away to her brother Laban's house in an attempt to save his life. Jacob worked many years for Laban in exchange for the hand of his daughter, Rachael. When the time for marriage came, he was given the wrong daughter, Leah, and still had to work another seven years to gain the hand of Rachael. Jacob's life, under Laban, seemed like a complete mess, a payback, one would think, for the deception he did to his brother, Esau. What good could come out of Jacob?

Jacob, however, was the father of the twelve tribes of Israel, and although the promise of Israel was given to Abraham, passed down to Isaac, who were both very upstanding in the sight of GOD, it was the seemingly devious Jacob, who was renamed "Israel" by GOD. GOD's promise to bless Israel, which HE had spoken to Abraham, was fulfilled through Jacob. The twelve tribes of Israel were the very sons of Jacob. Who would have thought that a man with such a controversial background would become so blessed by GOD? Who would have thought that a man, who covered himself in the skin of an animal to deceive his blind father, would gain favor from the LORD? *(See Genesis chapter 25:19 – chapter 35:26 for the story of Jacob.)*

It does not matter which road you got lost on, which web you became entangled in, when you submit to GOD and believe in HIM, HIS will for your life will be fulfilled. Just trust in HIM. Don't ever think you are not good enough.

Judah, the son of Jacob, had a son who was married to Tamar. Tamar's husband was evil in the sight of GOD, so GOD killed him. Judah sent his second son in to Tamar, to lay with her so that his deceased brother would have seed. Judah's second son did not like the fact that the children would not be his, so he let the semen spill on the ground. This displeased GOD, and GOD killed him also. Now Judah had another son, but afraid that his last son would also be killed, Judah sent Tamar back to the home of her family to wait until his younger son was old enough to be given to her.

The time had come and gone, Tamar was still at her family's home, and Judah did not keep his word concerning his youngest son. It happened that Judah visited Tamar's home town. Tamar heard of this and dressed herself like a prostitute and waited on her father-in-law. Judah slept with Tamar, not recognizing his daughter-in-law. Tamar got pregnant by Judah. Word went out to Judah that his daughter-in-law was pregnant, and he ordered them to have her killed. When Tamar revealed by whom she was pregnant, Judah realized he was responsible, he understood, and she was free. Well, from this act of deception that almost caused her death, Tamar had twins, Perez and Zerah, and descended from Perez, was King David, from David, Joseph was descended, the earthly father of JESUS CHRIST. Great things can come from anyone. *(See Genesis 38 for the story of Judah and Tamar.)*

GOD does not care where you came from. HE cares where you are going. Never allow Satan to make you feel like you are not good enough to be a soldier in the army of GOD. In you burns a flame that GOD finds very attractive, that flame is what HE is after. That flame is what GOD loves and from it HE can start a fire that brings honor to HIS name.

Day 17

"Ask, and it shall be given you; seek, and ye shall find; knock, and it shall be opened unto you: For every one that asketh receiveth; and he that seeketh findeth; and to him that knocketh it shall be opened."

Matthew 7:7-8

GOD gave me goosebumps.

On my life, this entire story is true. Nothing has been fabricated or exaggerated. Back in 1999 I made a grown up decision to move to Freeport. I had never lived in Freeport before and did not know anyone from there. I had never even lived on another Bahamian island. But, I wanted it, I wanted it really badly. So I prayed. I prayed, and I asked GOD to please help me move there, and I promised HIM, that once HE did, I would never miss church, do what is right, and live my life according to HIS will. I borrowed a fax machine and started faxing my CV to businesses in Freeport, mostly banks, as that is where my experience was. I called those businesses after and asked if those faxes were received, and, if they were hiring. Everyone seemed to be very discouraging. Grand Bahama, the island where Freeport exists, had been in a recession long before the rest of the country. Because of this, some of those business places added that not only were they not hiring, but no one else was in Grand Bahama. I didn't give up. I had always believed in GOD, and I had learned, even back then, before most of the miraculous events in my life, that GOD never fails!

My persistence and faith paid off, and, in less than a week, I had been hired by a Bank in Grand Bahama. The starting salary was just a little over $200 a week, $100 less than my last job paid in Nassau. But this is what I wanted. They said I was a stupid girl for making such a move. I didn't have the first dollar toward getting an apartment, I had no one to look after me, and I had never moved away from home. I didn't even own a car. I had never even traveled alone. This was a big step. But I always knew GOD never gives you anything half done. When GOD gives you something, HE gives you everything you need to sustain. I didn't get discouraged because I knew that GOD had answered my prayer and everything was going to be alright.

My father, who had come by to bring me a bin to put all of my belongings in, and put on the boat, had shown up shortly before my time to leave. He gave me $500.00. It was his paycheck for that week. I already had my ticket money, as a matter of fact, prior to getting his $500.00, ticket money was all I had. It was time to go! GOD was helping me. GOD gave me Goosebumps . . .

As I packed the night before my travels, I watched my brother's gold fish swimming around in the tank. He would come to the corner of the tank and watch me pack. I am watching him, watch me. Believe this, as I have written it, it is so very true. We had had that gold fish for five years by the time I was packing to move. My brother didn't do much for that fish. I did everything for the little guy. I cleaned his tank and made sure he was fed. I would even call from work and remind my brother to feed the fish if I could not make it. My heart has always been full of love and compassion for creatures. That gold fish had survived some really trying times himself. Some times the tank got so dirty, you would have to look over the top of it to see the fish. So now I'm packing, and ready to cry because of that gold fish. *Who is going to take care of him*, was all I was thinking. It was the very first thing that gave me any kind of doubts. The gold fish, I didn't want to leave the gold fish. Well, I went to bed, and woke up the next morning, the day I was to leave, and it relieved me to find, that some time during the night, the gold fish had died. It was time to go! GOD was pushing me. GOD gave me Goosebumps . . .

Well I made it to Freeport Sunday afternoon and had to be to work Monday morning. I used some of my father's $500 to get a room at a Hotel. Back then, I think it was around $100 a night. In five nights, I would have no paycheck and no money. But, I was not worried at all. We got paid once a month at the Bank, and even then, I doubt it would be enough for an apartment, light, transportation and food. The taxi I caught from the airport had taken it upon himself to give me free transportation to and from work, no questions asked. He just felt sorry for a young girl making a move like that with no one to run to. The transportation was sure appreciated and needed. GOD gave me Goosebumps . . .

Keeping true to my promise, I got back into my Word and stayed in my room Sunday night, reading my Bible and praising GOD for opening this door everyone said was locked. You don't know GOD! That morning as I'm getting ready for my first day of work, I spoke to GOD, and I told HIM, I would like to keep my word, but, I do not know where the church is or how I was going to get there. I said it, and forgot it. I went to work and started my training as a new teller. First customer of the morning, my first day at work, was Tamika. Tamika and I had both attended Bahamas Academy, but she had graduated a year earlier than me. Tamika had come to Western Union and had no idea I had just moved there. In school, we knew each other, but we weren't friends, so imagine my surprise when her face lit up to see me, and she asked, "How are you getting to church?" I told her I didn't know, unaware that she was now married to the head Pastor of one of our Churches, and from that day until I left Grand Bahama, I didn't have to worry about transportation to Church. GOD gave me Goosebumps...

By day three of my stay in Grand Bahama, my mother had sent me $1,400.00, that she got from the Credit Union, to help me with an apartment. GOD was helping me. GOD gave me Goosebumps...

An old friend of mine in Nassau had made an interesting phone call to the manager of another bank, who walked on my job and called me by name. He told me to come down and fill out an application for a car loan, but first, I had to find a car. I test drove a car a lady was selling for $2,000, but it was too hard to turn, and that, along with the fact that my salary wasn't much, was enough to discourage me from taking out a loan for a car. Well, even though I did not buy that car, there was surely a reason GOD introduced me to this lady. As I was down to the last $100.00 from my father, and not wanting to touch the money I had gotten from my mother, and still staying in this hotel, I was at work, and in my mind, I was a little worried, talking to GOD about time running out. True as GOD is real, right as I was thinking this, I got a phone call at work. It was the lady whose car I had test driven. She said, "I'm just calling to tell you not to worry, because I'm searching for an apartment for you." GOD gave me Goosebumps...

At the end of that work day, the lady called and said she would pick me up from work. She had an apartment for me to look at. We went to see this apartment, but it was already taken. The land-lady, however, had a large master bedroom with a private bath in her home which she said she would convert into an apartment for me. I moved into the room right away, and it was converted while I went to work. It turned out to be nicer and much larger than the original one, and, at $400 a month, it included light, water, cable, phone, and all the furnishings. GOD! GOD! GOD gave me Goosebumps...

Anyway, I'm resting easy at night now, but I am missing one thing. I don't have an iron. Listen, GOD will even throw in a bonus to tell you, even the little things HE will work out for you. I went to work and asked my coworkers if they knew where I could get an iron. They called some places, but none were close by. There was a Bed & Bath store right across the street, a little place. I asked their opinion on an iron being in there, and they told me straight out, "No!, you won't find an iron in there!" I walked in there anyway. I asked the lady, "Do you have an iron?" The lady looked at me, and I am not telling you a lie, she said, "Well praise the LORD . . ." she continued, "Miss, you see that iron sitting on that counter? I was just about to throw that out, and the LORD told me not to." I walked out there with the only iron in the shop which GOD told her to keep for me. GOD GAVE ME GOOSEBUMPS . . . You don't know GOD!

We are serving the very same miraculous GOD that reigned in the Bible. We just don't realize it because our life comes with no narration. I look at my Freeport experience, and I see no difference between the favor GOD has over my life and the favor HE gave to Jacob, Joseph, or Daniel. If ever I meet anyone who has doubts in the miracles of GOD, I tell them about my move to Freeport. Nothing was coincidental. This was, without a shadow of a doubt, all GOD. GOD IS REAL, and I take great pity on anyone who doesn't believe it. I love the LORD. You have no idea how my heart curves around my love for a GOD who has made time for me. May the LORD strike me dead if any of this story is false. This is just how it happened, back in 1999, when a young girl set out to make a big move with GOD in her heart and not a dollar in her pocket.

GOD is SO REAL!

Day 18

"And about the ninth hour JESUS cried with a loud voice, saying, 'Eli, Eli, lama sabachthani?' that is to say, 'MY GOD, MY GOD, why hast THOU forsaken ME?'"

Matthew 27:46

"Eli, Eli, lama sabachthani?"

Should GOD decide to bless me with a farm, I will hang these words at the very entrance. I have put them up as my online status from time to time, and those who know its meaning, "MY GOD, MY GOD, why hast THOU forsaken ME," usually send a note saying, "Katrina, GOD has not forsaken you." They don't understand why I put those words up there.

These were the heartbreaking words that JESUS cried out as HE hung on the cross, bleeding, sweating, crying, and suffering. My SAVIOR had been slaughtered and put on display, and even as HE hung dying, wisdom had not yet reached HIS accusers.

I put these words up as a reminder that what I have suffered in this life is nothing compared to what CHRIST had to endure. CHRIST who was a greater person than I could ever aspire to be, CHRIST who loved with a pure heart that only GOD HIMSELF could match, CHRIST who was so marvelous, that as HE hung on a cross made by HIS enemies, HE asked GOD to forgive them, CHRIST, the only begotten SON of GOD, suffered many things because of HIS love for us. These words are a reminder that GOD has not forsaken me.

We need to be reminded daily, as we go through our trials, that GOD has a purpose for our life, and HIS will, should we allow it, will be done. GOD can bring us through some very discouraging and humiliating things. In our dark moments, when the world looks at us with scorn, talks about us and laughs at our suffering while they seem to be elevating above us, we cry out to GOD and wonder why HE has allowed us to suffer this way. Sometimes, we come to believe that it is GOD who has brought this suffering on us. But it is only in our most devastating situations, when our enemies believe that they have laid us to rest, that GOD will be most glorified. GOD may give you the little blessings behind closed doors, but those big blessings will be put on display, so that the world will know and seek after the GOD you serve.

GOD has a strategy, and HIS strategy works. GOD knows that people love to watch us decline in life, and GOD knows that people love to talk about it. GOD knows how low we need to get in order for people to realize how great HE is. HE wants them to say, "I want to serve your GOD, because only a miracle could have brought you out of that dark place."

This is why I believe GOD allowed JESUS CHRIST to hang on a cross for all HIS enemies to see. As the curtains ripped in the Church, they said, "This MAN was truly the SON of GOD." Three days later, HE rose from HIS tomb. Who could perform such a miracle, but GOD? Now, HIS enemies know the GOD CHRIST represents, so much so, that right up to this present day, people who have never seen CHRIST are talking about the miracle GOD performed in raising HIM from death. That is evidence of what GOD can do. Had CHRIST not died on that cross, and risen again, the Word of GOD may not have been as powerful as it is today. We serve and believe in GOD today, because CHRIST hung on that cross, back then, thinking GOD had forsaken HIM. GOD has a plan.

When you see these words, "Eli, Eli, lama sabachthani?," be reminded that GOD has a plan, no matter how dark the place is now where you reside, GOD has a plan. HE has not forsaken you.

What is the worst thing you have ever come through in your life? Comparing your experience to the crucifixion of CHRIST, on a scale of 1-10, how bad does your experience measure up? How has it changed your life? How can your testimony change the life of others?

_____

_____

_____

_____

_____

_____

_____

_____

_____

_____

Day 19

"Now faith is the substance of things hoped for,
the evidence of things not seen."

Hebrews 11:1

If you think GOD isn't listening . . .

If you think GOD is not listening, I have a story or two for you. I lack patience. I am the most impatient person I know. If it isn't happening now, I am not interested and I am moving on. But I need patience in this life, especially for this farm I'm praying for, with all the helpless animals that will be roaming around, completely dependent on me. I need patience. So I prayed for it. I know I am not the only person who has heard people say, "Don't pray for patience." I'd like to add to that, an impatient person truly should not pray for patience. It is VERY TRUE what they say. GOD will try you. Oh YES HE WILL!

The first day I woke up praying for patience, here's what happened—true story. I was a caretaker for an elderly gentleman who is not allowed to drive, so, I had to drive him where he needed to go. He was usually in and out, honest to GOD, he was not a lingering man. He liked for me to take him to his boat so that he can do his checks. Usually, that was a ten minute stop. He was very considerate about keeping people waiting, and I often had to tell him, don't worry about me, I am fine. Well, we went to the boat, and, impatient me, expecting the usual ten minute trip, was in for a surprise. My gentleman not only stayed about 45 minutes on the boat, but he did it while I stood out in the sun, then the rain drizzled, then the sun, and like a true man being used by the LORD, he did not move. He decided that he was going to sit on his boat, relax, and neatly tie pieces of cord around the ends of all of his boat ropes. Now, those ropes could have gone home with him and he could have done that there. But, not when GOD was involved. I prayed for patience, well, let's get cracking.

Next day, it was to the grocery store with my gentleman, usually 15 minutes. He's consistently in and out with a few items. Well, he told me as we were going in to be patient because today he wanted to look around and see if he wanted anything else. That was a first. Did I mention I had been on that job almost six months at the time of this incident? And, I had never seen this.

Okay, next day, I was at the shipping company picking up my packages. Guess how long I was there just getting my invoices— about an hour and a half. OH LORD! You got me! I was very cranky, especially since there was a power issue the night before, and I went without electricity from 7:00 p.m. until 6:00 a.m. the next morning. Let me add, I wasn't waiting in line an hour and a half; I was in front of the customer service agent for that long, forwarding the same invoice. I had to do that a few times, and guess what? None of my packages were even ready, a first for me at this shipping company, which I have used for three years. I just knew praying for patience would do this to me.

This brings me to the time I am writing this. Before I placed all these devotions in a book, they were a part of my online blog. I went online intending to write a completely different blog, but, after having to sign in about thirty times, getting in about ten times, getting as far as my blog three times, and not being able to post a new blog, I thought, *I truly need to share my story of praying for patience and GOD's faithful answering.* Even then, while I was writing, for the first time ever, my host sent me a note saying, "We just updated the system and need to refresh," interrupting my blog entry. It was okay, because by now I was all smiles. YES LORD, I'M ON TO YOU. And, I am VERY GRATEFUL!

We are blessed to be able to approach the throne of grace, and still find favor in the sight of GOD, WHOM we have disappointed so many times. But, GOD IS FAITHFUL. So do not pray not expecting anything, because GOD is surely listening. I guarantee it.

Day 20

"Then shall they also answer him, saying, 'LORD, when saw we THEE an hungered, or athirst, or a stranger, or naked, or sick, or in prison, and did not minister unto THEE?' Then shall HE answer them, saying, 'Verily I say unto you, Inasmuch as ye did it not to one of the least of these, ye did it not to ME.'"

Matthew 25:44-45

Blessed to bless!

We do not give much thought, when we pray for a blessing, how selfish that prayer may be. Have you ever been in need of a meal, prayed to GOD, and someone gave you enough to feed a family of four? In your mind, you're thinking, *Wow, how GOD truly blessed me.* Did you ever think that maybe you were blessed not just for you, but for someone else in need?

In the beginning, when hardship first came my way, I found myself at the mercy of others. But, my pride and my disgust of being so needy, led me to deal with my suffering my own way. Just to go without. It did not kill me to miss a few meals and squash my dirty clothes on my hand with the soap I should have been bathing with. It did not kill me to bathe in a bucket. It did not kill me to sleep on a cold floor with no power and no running water. It did not kill me to live out of my car. It did not kill me, it made me stronger. It made me more aware. As a matter of fact, it killed me more to get help from others. The pride in me would rather struggle than be talked about.

Struggling brings awareness to those who are struggling. It helps you to understand the hunger in the eyes of someone whose pride is just too great to ask for a dollar. LORD, let me never forget my suffering, that suffering that will make me think twice about letting someone go hungry. I know what it is like to wish, if only for a drink of water, but to prefer to die than to ask. I have prayed that GOD would help me to be a blessing to others, and HE heard me.

When you have walked a long road of being needy, you see the blessing in being able to help someone else. However, anyone with a paycheck can give a little help, if the heart is willing. But some help requires less pride and more effort. One day, a lady's car broke down right across my gateway. I heard her trying to start it a couple times, then, she just sat there. I looked out from time to time because the cars would blow their horns behind her every time someone didn't notice she was broken down. It was a really nice car and she was nicely dressed. I heard her call someone on the phone. I thought to myself: *I'm not bothering, I cannot help her.* Then, I remembered my prayers. So, reluctantly, I walked out to the gate and asked if her blinkers were on. They were. I asked if she was out of gas; she didn't know. The gentleman I looked after had some gas in a container that he kept for his lawn mower, and I offered it to her. I could see that she was a little embarrassed sitting there, I knew the feeling. I had once sat on the side of the busy highway to the airport, in my broken down car, for about five hours before help came. Anyway, still thinking I'm no good to anyone, I got the gas. She had a chef's knife nicely wrapped in her car and one of those little, plastic juice bottles. After using her knife to cut the bottom out of the juice bottle, it made the perfect funnel to get the gas into the tank. Guess what? She started and went on her way, but not before offering me money that I did not take.

Seems like an everyday kind of thing, right? Here is why I think GOD had HIS hand in this. One, this lady tried to pay me. She could have afforded gas. Two, she broke down right in front of my gate, not a foot left or right, right in front of it. Three, I had the gas, and she had everything else we needed to get her sorted out. I believe GOD wanted to test me and see if I would be willing to help if HE blessed me enough to help someone, or, if I would be shy or think I am not good enough. Helping someone does not always come in a financial way. You will be surprised what little you can do that will make a big difference to someone else.

Now, here's the other part of my prayer. I told you this story to give you an example of how GOD can answer a prayer, as HE always does, and, to show how much help we can be without going into our pockets. But, I want to be someone who helps without boasting about it. I just want to feel it in my heart and be satisfied knowing that GOD is pleased, the person I helped is satisfied and, I just did something positive with my otherwise insignificant life. What good are we, if we cannot help someone else and spread the goodness of GOD? GOD will reward our acts of kindness with gifts man can never afford.

We should all aspire to be a blessing. Ask yourself if that person in need is a test from GOD. We may think, because we have known that person so long, or because we know the wrong they have done, that they are right to be suffering. But, could it be that their situation has just been a test to you for as long as you have known them? How long have you been failing?

How can you make a difference in the life of someone else? Is there someone in your life who has been crying for help, but you have ignored them? If you were in their position, would you wish someone could help you? What can you do today, without money, that can make someone a little more comfortable? Are you willing to help them? Going back down the lane of your life, can you think of someone, maybe even from your childhood, who seemed to always be in need? If they were a test, how did you score?

_____

_____

_____

_____

_____

_____

_____

_____

_____

Day 21

*"Blessed is the man that endureth temptation;
for when he is tried, he shall receive the crown of life,
which the LORD hath promised to them that love HIM."*

James 1:12

You've got a fan in Heaven!

Thousands of angels rejoice when one person gives their life to CHRIST. There is a celebration in heaven, every time GOD wins! Have you ever watched a game or even sat on the sidelines when someone you knew competed? Do you remember how good it felt when your team won, and the uproar from their fans just added to the excitement? Or, even greater, have you ever had the privilege of competing yourself, and remember how good you felt when the crowd cheered you on, how it just made you push harder? I wanted to let you know, that even though we cannot hear the excitement, someone is cheering you on daily.

I believe that after the initial celebration of our salvation, or even before, we are assigned an angel in Heaven. I believe our angel watches us daily, protecting us, helping to guide us, sharing with GOD all of our great accomplishments. I believe, when we give up, our angel cries. I truly believe that when we make it into the New Jerusalem, there will be at least one angel standing at the gate, waiting just for us. I truly believe it. I believe, just as we sit in front of the TV cheering on our favorite team, our angel in heaven, sits on the sidelines of our lives, cheering us on through every obstacle.

Only, to our angel, it is no game. Your angel knows that your very soul is the prize at stake. Your angel wants you to win.

As I am writing this, my eyes burn, because I am picturing an angel sitting alone by a river in heaven. It is a river of her very tears. She is crying because I gave up. She glances over from time to time at the other angels celebrating the victories of their humans, and her soul is aching. I broke her heart. She will not get another assignment, because GOD loves me so much, that HE will not give up on me, and neither will she. Until the day I die, she will push, and cheer, and whisper encouraging words, in hopes that one day she can join in the celebration with the other angels. She wants so badly to tell GOD some good news. GOD sits and watches her cry. It has been so long since HE has seen her smile. Her tears, her sadness, her disappointments are all because of me. She is not alone. There are other angels crying in corners of heaven. I am not the only one who disappoints my biggest fan.

I want to inspire us all to get back up, rejoin the race. The voice in your head that pushes you is not always your own. You've got a fan in heaven! Give your fan something to celebrate. Give your angel a reason to get out of that lonely corner and smile. Believe that there is at least one angel in heaven cheering you on. Don't give up! Hold on! Fight! The prize is eternal life, and to sit at a dinner table with GOD!

Day 22

"Be careful for nothing; but in everything
by prayer and supplication with thanksgiving
let your requests be made known unto GOD."

Philippians 4:6

Be specific when you pray!

I am going to tell you two true stories that proved to me that we need to be very specific when we pray.

Back in 2005 I set out to put on my own Stage Play. I wrote it and directed it. It had long been a dream of mine to be a successful actress, and since I did not have the connections to get myself lined up with anything, I thought, *Let me do my own thing.* I was very excited about putting on my first play, and like everything else in my life, I put it before GOD. I prayed. I told GOD I wanted my name to be famous, I wanted to hear it everywhere. Perhaps you can already see where this is going.

True story, I got a sponsor for my radio ad and did all of the fliers and other publications by myself, except for the tickets. The weekend that the play was scheduled, Hurricane Katrina threatened to hit Nassau. I rescheduled, even though Hurricane Katrina came nowhere near us and nothing but sunshine could be seen that weekend. However, there was no money to advertise again and hardly anyone knew about the change in the play date. The play flopped, big time. The under twenty people who showed up were all relatives of the cast members and me. We had done so much running around that day that one of my cast members fell out at the end, right when they called my name. She had not had anything to eat. The little money I made, I had to feed them. I walked away, not breaking even, but owing. However, it has been over ten years, and the world would not stop talking about Hurricane Katrina. I am so sick of hearing my name! Hurricane Katrina became so popular that she got her own television station. With all the earthquakes, tornadoes, tsunamis and other tragedies that took place thereafter, Hurricane Katrina is still the most talked about disaster in the world today. My name is famous and everyone knows it. That was not what I meant GOD, next time I will make it clearer.

I knew then that I needed to be specific with my prayers, but I forgot. In 2013 I wrote out my resolutions and was determined to make them come true, as many as I could. I have done pretty well so far, but there are a few I would like to focus on. I had never been on a cruise, I had never visited a U.S. state, other than Florida, and I had never been to another Caribbean country, other than home, in The Bahamas. So I booked myself on a cruise to Mexico. That was going to knock out two resolutions. I prayed that GOD would make this the most memorable vacation ever. It was my first real vacation and everything was paid for in advance.

True story, I got on the cruise, alone. Everything was closed except the casino. I had promised I would not gamble, but, with no one to talk to, it was the only thing to do. Losing, nothing else to do, cruise sucks! I had been online bragging to the cruise line's page about my upcoming first cruise ever, so naturally they wanted to know how it was going. I told them I felt the cruise was so boring that I wished I could jump off. Well, let me tell you, certain words you do not use when you are cruising out to sea. They took that as a suicide threat. They were terrified. I will not tell you all the measures they took for my safety, because I am not quite ready to laugh at that part yet.

I will tell you that I am now banned from that cruise line for life. They were very nice and private about it, assigned me a nice agent and paid my way home, even though they would not refund a penny of my money, despite the fact that I had only spent one day on the ship. Well, when we reached Mexico, they let me off with a gentleman who helped me the whole way. I must say, I was terrified to be in Mexico under those conditions. I had heard many horror stories about that part of the world. I kept my bag very close to me, and still checked it before going through security to make sure the spirit of a Mexican did not put drugs in it. I was so relieved when that plane took off. I had a connection flight from Mexico to Texas and then on to Orlando.

Well, I went on my first cruise, saw another Caribbean country (Mexico), and visited another U.S. State (Texas), and IT IS THE MOST MEMORABLE VACATION EVER. I will never forget being banned from my first cruise line, especially since I have a nice letter that proves it. That was not what I meant GOD, but I see YOU smiling.

Do not take for granted that HE is GOD and knows exactly what you want. Be very specific when you pray.

No matter how foolish it may sound to you, or how badly you hope no one else would ever see it, take that prayer that you have put before GOD, write it here, only this time, include the little details you think HE already knows. One day, you may reflect back here and discover that even those little things, HE took care of.

_____

_____

_____

_____

_____

_____

_____

_____

_____

_____

_____

Day 23

"Him that overcometh will I make a pillar in the temple of MY GOD, and he shall go no more out: and I will write upon him the name of MY GOD, and the name of the city of MY GOD, which is New Jerusalem, which cometh down out of heaven from MY GOD: and I will write upon him MY new name."

Revelation 3:12

Then, I imagine Heaven!

To me, life feels like a race with no view of the finish line. Every turn seems to bring a new obstacle, and sometimes I feel unprepared to conquer it. With this life comes no training, no manual. I don't hear the voices cheering me on; I feel like I am running this all alone. Life is not a fairy tale. We think we can predict the next event, but most times we are wrong. Sometimes I feel like I am running in circles. I've seen this obstacle before. It seems, when I take another route in the race, to avoid the mountains I don't feel strong enough to climb, I only find them again in the pathways I thought were safe. Sometimes I feel like giving up. Sometimes I feel like it would be easier to let go of GOD and live my life in sin. I feel like maybe Satan would not bother me so much. Maybe the obstacles would move. But then, I imagine heaven!

I imagine the day when I can see the finish line. I imagine the voices of thousands of angels cheering me on, "You're almost there, Katrina." They know my name. I imagine their genuine smiles. They really care about my victory. I imagine Daniel, Jacob, Isaac, Abraham, just glowing and smiling and waving me in. I imagine GOD with tears in HIS eyes. HE knows the woman about to cross that line has had an insane journey. I imagine how happy HE would be to tell me all about my life, and how proud HE is that I have turned around. OH, LORD, how I imagine heaven! I imagine sitting down with my SAVIOR, unable to get out my praise, because the tears will not stop flowing. I imagine all my pride leaving my body when I scream "HALLELUJAH!" I imagine lying down on those streets of gold, surrounded by all of my brothers and sisters in CHRIST. I imagine staying up from sunrise to sunrise, just talking about how we thought we would never make it in. I imagine the angels, celebrating. There is an angel there who has been waiting a lifetime to sit with me. I imagine how happy she will be the day I am safe in my FATHER's arms. OH, LORD, how I imagine heaven!

I imagine what it would be like to sit down with Moses, and hear the firsthand account of the journey out of Egypt. I imagine Noah, telling the children how he felt when the rain waters lifted the Ark from the foundation of the earth. I imagine CHRIST showing us the piercings in HIS hands. They could have healed, but HE kept them, just for us. I imagine Daniel walking down those golden streets with lions at his side. I imagine Jacob in a corner, smiling. He is an old man, frozen in time, but he still has that walking stick, a glorious adornment of where he's journeyed from. I imagine Joseph with his coat of many colors. He hasn't worn it for a while, but today is a special day, and he wanted everyone to see him in it. He tells me he has seen me in his dreams. OH, LORD, I do imagine heaven!

I imagine the milk and honey, flowing just like they said it would. We break out in song, and everyone knows the words. All of our loved ones who have gone on before us, those that were saved, I see them all around us. They've never looked better. No sign of sickness in heaven. I imagine the way GOD smiles when I ask HIM, "LORD, what was the fruit on the Tree of Life?" I imagine heaven will have many surprises, and no more obstacles.

I imagine heaven, and so I continue to press on. What a waste of life to have had such a painful and trying journey, and never get to see a smile from my SAVIOR. I don't want my first sight of HIM to be HIS face in disappointment. I don't want to hear HIM say, "Depart from me, I know you not!" I don't want to imagine that.

Continue to press on! Don't give up! Heaven is a beautiful end to this turbulent journey.

Day 24

"And JESUS called a little child unto HIM,
and set him in the midst of them, And said,
'Verily I say unto you, Except ye be converted,
and become as little children, ye shall not enter
into the kingdom of heaven. Whosoever therefore
shall humble himself as this little child, the same
is greatest in the kingdom of heaven.'"

Matthew 18:2-4

I saw an angel!

If we could go back to the innocence of our childhood, back when our beliefs were not within the barriers of what seems rational, how beautiful life would be. When I was just a little girl I found a four-leaf clover, just one time. I have never seen one again, and I do look. I can remember wishing on a shooting star when my mother went away, for a doll. She brought that doll back when she came, even though before she left she told me that I was not getting any more dolls. I still believe in shooting stars, but I have not had any of my wishes come true since my childhood. Growing up can be destruction to our faith.

Until I was nine years old, I wet the bed. My grandmother would make a bed on the floor for me whenever I slept at her house. Well, one night, when I was about five or so, I was lying on my floor bed, and I looked up in the ceiling. There was an angel, spread diagonally up there. I remember it well, and I know it was not a dream. She had her right hand spread to the bottom left corner of the ceiling, from the position I was lying. Her feet were at the top right, and her left hand was down along her side. She was looking right at me. Her complexion is unclear to me, but I know her wings and the dress she wore all blended in. They were cream colored.

This was not the tiny, cute kind of angel that would live in a child's imagination. This was a grown woman, an adult watching over me. It is heartbreaking sometimes to think that I no longer see the things I did when I was a child. It comes with the realization that I have allowed something to come between GOD and me. What we do and think about the symbols of blessings when we become adults must be so hurtful to GOD. I know HE remembers when we could see an angel and feel at peace. Then we lost hope and now, seeing an angel may make national news, banishing any hope of GOD with all the scientific babble and carnal rationalizing.

When we become adults, and get a taste of this life and this world, we become more separate from GOD. We need to become like little children again. How I wish I could see angels now, even though as a woman, my mind may not receive it as I did in the innocence of my childhood.

I do not have the option of believing that GOD does not exist, because before I really knew HIM, the events in my life testified of HIM. I just really wanted to share this story that I have not told many people, but have held close to my heart, reliving it as often as I can, hoping that GOD will one day see me as a child again.

Day 25

"For we wrestle not against flesh and blood,
but against principalities, against powers,
against the rulers of the darkness of this world,
against spiritual wickedness in high places.
Wherefore take unto you the whole armour of GOD,
that ye may be able to withstand in the evil day,
and having done all, to stand."

Ephesians 6:12-13

Winner gets your soul!

I don't think we have the slightest idea how serious this life is that we are living. I think we have some fairy tale notion in our heads, and we seem to think that no matter how we play the hand we've been dealt, we are safe in the game. I feel sorry for us, and the way we think. We are caught in the middle of a war, a war for our very soul. Our soul is in a pot, winner takes all. This is real life. We are not guaranteed a happy ending, this is not the movies.

We seem to think we are living in comfortable times. How bad must it get before we realize that we are in trouble? How terrible do you expect the end times to become? With natural disasters at every corner of the world, wars and rumors of wars, the slaughtering of Christians, the escorting of prayer from our schools, how can we even question the times we currently live in? This is not a future prediction. This is what we are presently living in. I am expecting the heavens to roll open like a scroll within my lifetime. I am expecting the rapture . . . expecting it, but am I prepared for it?

Every day, every move, every word, we make a decision. We choose a side. Our actions and the way we live our life is either securing our soul in heaven or planting it in hell. Who will win our souls? Whose team are we playing for? We need to get back in the Word of GOD, because somewhere down the line, we began to believe that if the law allows it, it is righteous. The law is allowing for things that GOD does not approve of. Learn the difference, know the difference. It is a matter of life or death.

Also, we have become so comfortable in our sins that we just accept them as a part of our character. We have lost our will to conquer evil and secure our salvation. At some point, it seems we gave up. We stopped trying to do what is right. We have accepted everything that is wrong with the world.

One of the biggest problems we are experiencing, in my opinion, is the church making allowances for sin. Because the church does not want to lose their members, they will not touch on topics that will cost them that tithe envelope. Be careful who you let feed your spirit. Each man needs to learn the Word of GOD for himself. Those of us who stand on the side of GOD, need to be bold in spirit, and speak up against what we know is wrong. Satan has become very bold in his approach. Satan has become so bold that he has taken people who are openly committing an abomination against GOD, and made them head of the church. Then we, who are called soldiers of CHRIST, sit quietly, and talk about it behind the backs of those we do not want to offend. It is not a matter of offending anyone. It is a matter of helping to save our brother and sisters from the clutches of Satan. We are not helping them by letting them go down that dark path; we are hurting them, and YES, we are responsible.

There is guaranteed a day when the LORD will return. We need to realize that every moment we are heading toward that day. There will not be another chance after that. We may not be the ones doing the wrong, but, we may be the ones put in the path to help our brothers and sisters, therefore we have a responsibility. It may not be a matter of helping to correct their actions. We may be leading by poor example. First, before you attempt to correct anyone or help steer them in the right direction, make certain you are not driving on the wrong side of the highway. Let it begin with us. Let the world see the change in us.

Let us continue to encourage each other. From this day forth, as you go through your life, take a good look at the path you are walking. Are you really heaven-bound? Do you even know? How well do you know the Word of GOD? Let us pray for each other and help each other. Read the Word of GOD. Get to know what is expected of your life, before it is too late. Take a good look at your performance, your character. Who is winning your soul? And, are you standing by and watching the souls of your loved ones end up in the wrong pot? Let us remain vigilant. Do not accept the way of the world, believing that GOD is no more. GOD remains and HIS day approaches. Is HE winning your soul?

Use this time and space to weigh out the good and bad in your character. I'm dreading doing this exercise myself. Take a good look at how you live daily. Then, see how many of those bad characteristics you are ready to eliminate right away. That is really going to make Satan angry. How much does the enemy have over you? How much of your time does he play a part in? Are you ready to evict him from your life? What are some good characteristics you can use to replace the bad characteristics in you?

_____

_____

_____

_____

_____

_____

_____

_____

_____

_____

Day 26

"The young man saith unto HIM, 'All these things have I kept from my youth up: what lack I yet?' JESUS said unto him, 'If thou wilt be perfect, go and sell that thou hast, and give to the poor, and thou shalt have treasure in heaven: and come and follow ME.' But when the young man heard that saying, he went away sorrowful: for he had great possessions.

Then said JESUS unto HIS disciples, 'Verily I say unto you that a rich man shall hardly enter into the kingdom of heaven. And again I say unto you, It is easier for a camel to go through the eye of a needle, than for a rich man to enter into the kingdom of GOD.' When HIS disciples heard it, they were exceedingly amazed, saying, 'Who then can be saved?' But JESUS beheld them, and said unto them, 'With men this is impossible; but with GOD all things are possible.'"

Matthew 19:20-26

The curse of riches!

I find it quite interesting the way spiritual leaders who know the Word of GOD, continue to preach riches to their congregation. It seems that with every promise of wealth from spiritual leaders comes a call for the planting of a seed, give money to get money. It's unfortunate that the heads of the church have taken advantage of the desperation of their parishioners, while preaching something contrary to the Word of GOD.

We all wish we didn't have financial burdens. We need to pray to be comfortable rather than wealthy. We all need something to keep us on our knees, because the sad reality is, without having a need, some of us would not even pray. Poor people pray more than anyone else, I truly believe that. I also believe that GOD keeps us in need to keep us humble. How appreciative is someone who does not know the pain of sacrifice and the value of answered prayers?

Do not be taken in by the gimmick of seed planting for riches. It is like digging your way to hell. Every seed is a shovel full of dirt. With all the seeds some of you have planted, you could have been rich already. Plant your seeds in the life of someone in need, those unfortunate people who don't have enough to plant a seed of their own. Plant your seeds in the church for the benefit of the assembly, not for anything in return.

> *"Let the brother of low degree rejoice in that he is exalted: But the rich, in that he is made low: because as the flower of the grass he shall pass away. For the sun is no sooner risen with a burning heat, but it withereth the grass, and the flower thereof falleth, and the grace of the fashion of it perisheth: so also shall the rich man fade away in his ways." (James 1:9-11)*

What is the need to be rich? What would you do with all the extra money you do not need? Take a very close inventory of your life. What do you want that you do not have? Ask yourself, if you had all the things you wanted, how much time would be shaved off your sessions with GOD? Will your prayers then become limited to, "Thank YOU, LORD, for life?" An honest assessment of how your life may change if you had every single thing you are praying for, may very well tell you why GOD has held a blessing or two back from you.

My FATHER is very jealous and HE will tolerate no rivals. HE already knows what your life would be like with the things you are asking for. HE also knows what you need before you even ask. HE knows what is right for your life and your future. HE knows when it is enough. Besides, what about you is so special that you should be excluded from the struggles of life? JESUS CHRIST had nothing but the clothes on HIS back. When they hung my SAVIOR on the cross, they didn't even give HIM the dignity of HIS attire. They gambled for HIS clothing while HE hung, dying. Nothing you can acquire in this world can be taken with you when you leave, and, no earthly thing can save you.

"Let your conversation be without covetousness; and be content with such things as ye have: for HE hath said, 'I will never leave thee, nor forsake thee.' So that we may boldly say, 'The LORD is my helper, and I will not fear what man shall do unto me.'" (Hebrews 13:5-6)

Can we even be satisfied? Everyone in this world has something more they want. The more they have, the more they want. When is it enough? Let us pray for comfort in life, that GOD would supply all that we NEED, not all that we WANT. Do not let the FATHER return and find you on your knees praying for something that will not get you in to the New Jerusalem.

If you had all the money you have ever wanted, what would you do with it, and, how much of your spending would be offensive to the FATHER? How would wealth change your life? How would it affect your relationship with GOD? Now ask yourself, do you need all the money you would like to have, or can you live comfortably without it?

Day 27

"Peace I leave with you, my peace I give unto you:
not as the world giveth, give I unto you.
Let not your heart be troubled,
neither let it be afraid."

John 14:27

GOD gave me peace!

People find it hard to believe some of the situations I've survived. Because I've lived it, I wonder what is so unbelievable about it. There are times when I don't want to share it, because they are some humiliating situations I have risen from, but one thing leads to another in a conversation. I have shared my stories with some people, and I wish I could take them back. Those carnal minds cannot navigate through nor understand the goodness of GOD. They just see gossip's opportunities brewing. In the end, I guess it is up to us if we focus on what they are likely to talk about from our past behind our backs, or, if we are going to continue to testify to the goodness of GOD. I say keep spreading the good news, tell the world how far the LORD has brought you from.

As I lived daily in my trying situations, I found comfort and peace. What someone else would cry every day in, I found something to sing about. I have the gift of turning lemons into lemonade. GOD gives me peace. I never really thought about it, the way I'm thinking about it now. Looking back over my life, I found peace right in the middle of hell's playground. I found peace living out of my tiny car, even when it broke down, with all my stuff, on the side of a busy highway. I found peace in a one room shack, with no plumbing. I found peace living in a storage container, infested with roaches, frogs, and snakes, without anything to eat.

I now realize that I am a strong woman. I have endured a lot of hardship, and I am just fine. I am doing just fine. I can remember getting out of some situations and saying, I pray I never go back there, then finding my way back there, and still, doing just fine. It never killed me. It didn't even break me down. It really built me up. I know that it was GOD.

GOD must have sent HIS comforting angels to surround and protect me. GOD gave me peace. Every day, I had something to be grateful for, even in those places where everything seemed to be going wrong, I found something to be grateful for.

Sometimes, when we are down and out, we cry too much, throw such a big pity party, that we don't even notice that we have the strength to sit right in the midst of torment, and be at peace. If we would just sit still and be silent, we would feel the comforting hand of GOD carrying us, in our darkest moments, when we feel too weak to carry ourselves.

I don't know what you may be going through right now, but I know that someday, it will be a memory. Do not take the burden of your present obstacle into the beauty of your future. Endure what you must, pray for strength, let it strengthen you. GOD will give you peace, just let HIM. A captain cannot brag about being a good navigator until he has sailed a ship through a really bad storm. In other words, you should not measure your faith and strength in GOD by the way you can hold on when things are going well. It is how well you survive when hell is surrounding you. Can you handle the heat? Can you sit still and be at peace when your surroundings are far from peaceful? Can you trust and praise GOD when your situation feels like HE's abandoned you?

The peace that GOD has promised us is not what we feel when

all is well. It is the calmness in our spirits when our souls should feel tormented.

What if GOD does not intend to bring you out of your most trying situation? What if GOD's plan is to leave you there until you appreciate where you are? You think you cannot endure it, but while you are crying and complaining, you are enduring it, you just don't want to. When you next find yourself in a situation you feel you cannot endure, be still. You are stronger than you know, and GOD's peace is a more faithful promise and a more valuable gift than being taken out of torment. As GOD has been faithful to give me peace in the midst of my storms, I am certain HE will be just as faithful to all who serve HIM. Just be still.

Reflect here on a situation you went through that someone else seemed to have great difficulty with. Can you think of something that you felt was difficult while you were enduring it, but then came out of it and realized, it wasn't so bad? If you had to face the same situation again, how would you handle it differently?

_____
_____
_____
_____
_____
_____
_____
_____
_____
_____
_____

Day 28

*"For THOU, LORD, wilt bless the righteous;
with favour wilt THOU compass him as with a shield."*

Psalm 5:12

GOD's favor!

When something good you never believed could happen to you, actually occurs, I call that a miracle. When something good seemed more likely to be granted to someone more deserving, and ended up in your hands, I call that favor!

The whole purpose of the fast that inspired this book was the farm I am praying to my FATHER for. I don't know what a farm would be without a mango tree. I love mangoes. I don't know anyone who doesn't. I don't have a mango tree where I live, but I wanted to plant mango seeds. I asked everyone I knew to save their mango seeds for me.

One day, while I was on this fast, I went out for my morning jog, and stumbled across one of those big, juicy, yellow and red mangoes, in the middle of nowhere, no trees nearby. *This was clearly the work of the LORD*, I thought to myself. *HE is showing me that HE can provide all that I need, if I just ask.* I was fasting so I could not enjoy the mango, but I cut it open, took the seed, and gave the fruit away. Then GOD blessed my appreciation for that one seed with more mango seeds than I could plant. I had more seeds than I could handle. At one point I planted about twenty seeds. Among those twenty seeds was the seed of what we Bahamians call, a "Hairy Mango." They are sweet but annoying. They get stuck in your teeth. I felt bad for being ungrateful for it. I really could not care less if that one grew or not.

About two weeks after my mass mango seed planting, one of them started to sprout. Wouldn't you know it? It was that one "Hairy Mango" that I could not care less about. She became the light in my eyes. I took photos of her daily because she grew so beautifully. As a matter of fact, she became my "Miracle Mango Tree." She grew five sprouts from that one seed. She was a marvel. I could not believe it.

GOD was showing me, that the very one that I rejected, was the one to bring me joy. She, my "Miracle Mango Tree," had found favor in GOD's eyes, when HE realized that she was not loved. Out of the twenty seeds I planted, she was the only one that grew. After a while, the sprouts started to die off. She was left with only two. But while I fasted for 40 days, those sprouts remained strong. As a matter of fact, two years later, she is the only seed I planted during my 2014 fast that is still going strong and healthy. GOD used this little mango tree to teach me a very valuable lesson. With GOD's favor, all things are possible, to those that believe. I believe. I truly do.

My mango tree reminds me of the story of Leah. *"And when the LORD saw that Leah was hated, HE opened her womb: but Rachel was barren. And Leah conceived, and bare a son, and she called his name Reuben: for she said, 'Surely the LORD hath looked upon my affliction; now therefore my husband will love me.'" (Genesis 29:31-32)*

Leah bore Jacob four sons before anyone else opened their wombs for him. Unfortunately, Jacob was too in love with Rachael to even appreciate that the favor of GOD was on the wife he didn't seem to love.

How do you identify GOD's favor? When three of the four ropes your life hangs on have given away, and that last rope has been holding you so long that the entire world stands in amazement, that's GOD's favor! When you are down to your last dollar and somehow everything you need comes your way, and you still have that last dollar, unspent, that's GOD's favor! Favor is evident when you should be losing, but you keep coming out on top. A miracle is when it happens. Favor is when it will not stop happening.

Favor comes to those who are faithful and humble. When you can acquire the blessings of the LORD without throwing it arrogantly in the faces of others, you will find GOD's favor in your life. GOD's favor is like walking around with miracles in your pocket—use one when needed. Daily I am praying for favor. It's that mango tree that never goes out of season, always bearing, always sweet.

Can you think of something you received that you didn't expect because you felt someone else was more likely to receive it? Or, is there something you are currently praying for that you feel may be a bit out of your reach? Write it here, put it before GOD, then next to it, write "favor." Should it be the will of the FATHER that you receive that blessing, you will one day look back and see that it was GOD's "favor" that ushered you to the front of that line.

_____
_____
_____
_____
_____
_____
_____
_____
_____
_____

Day 29

*"Set a watch, O LORD, before my mouth;
keep the door of my lips."*

Psalm 141:3

LORD, post a guard at the gate of my lips!

It is so easy to get caught up in gossip. I am praying always that GOD would remove any desire from me that loves to gossip. The Bible tells us that gossiping is something that GOD hates. The sad part about it is that gossiping is a most common pastime among church folks. We seem to think because we're talking about people who are doing wrong, it's O.K., but it isn't. It's never O.K. to sit and discuss people and their affairs that do not concern us. If you have discomfort with your sisters and brothers, talk to them about it. It is not beneficial to the kingdom if we talk about them.

> *"A froward man soweth strife: and a whisperer separateth chief friends." (Proverbs 16:28)*

There is a very popular and true saying, "What you give to the world, you cannot take back." We must be so careful what we say in our moments of anger and distress. We must be so careful how we talk about others. What it takes us a second to say, it takes a lifetime for the world to forget.

> *"Whoso keepeth his mouth and his tongue keepeth his soul from troubles." (Proverbs 21:23)*

When we are angry with our friends, our family, our love-partners, we always feel the need to vent to someone. In our anger, we give the world the ammunition to later destroy us. When our anger and pain has subsided and we are ready to move forward with our lives, the world will not let us forget the things we said in our vulnerable moments. Our mouths give us more regret than anything else. This is especially the case with an emotional woman. We must learn to hold our peace until the anger subsides and we can speak rationally.

For married people, your business should never be a public discussion, angry or not. With your angry lips you invite people into your marriage, people you know do not belong there. Do you know the comfort you bring to the world when they realize that you are unhappy? Do you know how far the flaws of your union will travel by the time you have reconciled with your partner? Unless your marriage has become an abusive trap and you need help for your safety, your marital problems should remain in your marriage. If not, certainly you will have regrets. The same should be said about any relationship where trust should exist, be it friendships or family, unless you are seeking the help of someone, in honesty and not with spite, your business should not be broadcast. There is a lot to be said about people who enjoy hearing your bad news, and sit anxiously to receive it.

> *"Thou shalt not go up and down as a talebearer among thy people: neither shalt thou stand against the blood of thy neighbour: I am the LORD." (Leviticus 19:16)*

Be very careful with people who bring gossip; they also carry gossip. And those of us who may not engage in the actual speaking of the gossip, are just as guilty when we listen to it. We fuel the fire. If a gossiper has no audience, there will be no gossip. Learn to speak out against gossip and let people know that you don't want to hear it. People will feel free to gossip to you for one of two reasons; either you are always willing to listen, or, they have heard enough about you to know that you will enjoy what they have to say. Think about that the next time you find yourself as the audience in someone's gossip. Ask yourself, "What about me makes this person so comfortable to talk about others with me?"

"These six things doth the LORD hate: yea, seven are an abomination unto HIM: A proud look, a lying tongue, and hands that shed innocent blood, an heart that deviseth wicked imaginations, feet that be swift in running to mischief, a false witness that speaketh lies, and he that soweth discord among brethren." (Proverbs 6:16-19)

I know how sweet the sound of hearing someone's downfall can be. For some of us, unfortunately, it makes us feel better about ourselves to tear down others, or to see others being torn down. If it makes you feel better about yourself to see the destruction of someone else, your heart is not at all what a heart of GOD should be. We should delight in seeing good happen to others. Gossip is exciting, but we have to refrain from it if we are going to be of good character. Stand up and walk away from it. Nothing good can come out of gossiping.

"Death and life are in the power of the tongue: and they that love it shall eat the fruit thereof." (Proverbs 18:21)

This tongue that wags in our heads can be used for so much good. But we use it to lie, backbite, tear down, belittle, and completely destroy the life and character of others. What part of the New Jerusalem do you think you will be sitting in talking about people behind their backs? Build better character, work toward better character now. You think on this topic and your enemies come to mind. But it is always the ones closest to us who set out to destroy us. They are the ones that talk about us, and the ones we talk about, because they are the ones we are close enough to know about.

I have never heard my enemies say the filth about me that those closest to me have said. I know the destruction of the tongue. The tongue has landed me close to depression, but blessed I am, for GOD kept me sane. Some do not make it out. This tongue has caused wars, suicides, false imprisonment, and even murder. Being a victim of negative gossip makes me think long and hard about people who bring gossip. One thing I often consider is that the story is usually told in the favor of the gossiper, and most times, it is not the whole truth. I instantly lose respect for anyone who claims to be of GOD and brings a story about someone. It is confusing. Some of us hate being talked about, yet we will entertain conversations about others. If you give the fruit of gossip, expect to eat the fruit of gossip, and a sour fruit it is. Trust me, I know.

This is my prayer, to walk away from gossip and to encourage everyone else to walk away and refrain from it. Yes, I have used this tongue for the wrong purpose and I have enjoyed hearing the destruction of my enemies. I was wrong. We were wrong when we talked about our enemies, our friends or our relatives, regardless of who we were talking to or what they had said about us. We were wrong when we clicked "share" on those social networks and contributed to the destruction of someone's character. We were wrong when we sat and listened while someone tore down someone else. We were wrong. And, we thought we were clever when we started the conversation with, "I don't like to gossip, but . . ." or "Not talking about people, but . . ." We were wrong, but thank GOD for conviction, because now we can get right.

One of the most powerful things JESUS ever said was *"And as ye would that men should do to you, do ye also to them likewise." (Luke 6:31).* JESUS did not say, do to men as they have already done to you. No matter what wrong people have committed against us, we need to be certain that we are doing what is right in the sight of the LORD. Are any of our offenders worth our salvation? Be very careful the seeds you sow in this life. If you sow seeds of gossip, you will reap seeds of gossip. Don't plant a seed whose fruits you cannot stand the taste of. The LORD does not like gossip one bit. We are asked to be CHRIST-like, and CHRIST does not gossip.

Day 30

"*Confirming the souls of the disciples,
and exhorting them to continue in the faith,
and that we must through much tribulation
enter into the kingdom of GOD.*"

Act 14:22

Troubling waters!

I was 15 years old when I first gave my life to CHRIST. It was a week of prayer at my High School and they made the usual altar call. It was not the first time I had answered that call, but something about this time was different. The times I had stood before were just for show, or because my friends were standing. This time, I did it because GOD was watching and I wanted HIM to know that I was ready. I can remember the Pastor saying, "You don't have to be perfect. Come to GOD just as you are." That is what made the difference for me, realizing that I did not have to be perfect.

Even at that young age, life was a bit much for me. I expected that giving my life to GOD would now make the difference, and things would get better, easier. In the beginning, it seemed like GOD was working overtime in my life, bringing me some comfort.

I can remember walking along my Christian path, that smooth, paved, and well-lit journey. Then there came the speed bumps. I was not detoured, they presented no obstacles. I saw those as an opportunity to be strengthened. Further down my journey, some of those speed bumps got higher and higher, until they became mountains. I was not detoured. I had been going over the bumps for a while and the fact that they gradually got bigger prepared me well for greater obstacles.

I had mastered the speed bumps and mountains in my journey by the time I came to my first pot hole. It was not enough to detour me, but, it did confuse me slightly. I didn't expect pot holes in this journey. There had only been speed bumps and mountains until now. Those pot holes were small enough to step over, but big enough to leave me concerned. The speed bumps and mountains were consistent by now. The pot holes were very rare, so rare that it left me distraught for a while every time I had to step over one. Just when I thought I would not see them anymore, another one would appear.

The speed bumps and mountains continued as I reached the point in my journey where, although infrequent, the appearance of the pot holes was expected. I no longer got confused by them. I took them in the same stride as I did the speed bumps and mountains. The pot holes became more frequent and just as I had fully prepared myself for them, they got wider and deeper. They got so big that I could not just step over them anymore, I had to go around. It was not enough to discourage me, until I found myself at those points where the pot holes were right at the break of the mountains I had to climb. It made my journey so much longer, such a task to conquer one obstacle only to find myself right in the midst of another.

The frequency of the usual obstacles, the speed bumps, mountains, and large pot holes became very familiar and as time went by, I looked forward to overcoming them all, until it started to rain. Something about being soaked in one obstacle made all the other obstacles feel different. Those speed bumps I bounced over, that mountain I ran over, and those pot holes I no longer thought twice about felt really hard, really trying, just too much to bear when I was wet with something else I could not handle. I started to feel the frustration and discouragement of a woman trying to follow the path of GOD.

The rain falling alone was not enough to detour me, but the rain falling while I needed to focus on other obstacles was a little more than I felt prepared to conquer. Instead of running over the mountains and around the large pot holes, I would just stand there, watching the waters fill those pot holes. The spirit that drove me to dance over my obstacles seemed to have left me. I lost my motivation. If GOD would only stop the rain, I would be fine with the other trials.

At that point in my Christian walk, I didn't want to try to overcome the rain. I felt that I had done so well with the other challenges that I should be rewarded, not tormented. Something in me knew that overcoming this obstacle would bring greater obstacles, and, I was just not ready for that. It was not fair. "LORD," I prayed, "when is it going to get easier?"

Sick and tired of standing there, in the rain, realizing it was not getting easier and the rain was persisting, I proceeded. In the rain, I went over the speed bumps and mountains, then around the pot holes. After a while, the rains did not bother me. I overcame every obstacle just I had before, in the rain . . . until the pot holes became huge sink holes, flooded with rain. I could not go around them because I could not tell where they started or ended. I turned around and headed back.

Heading in the wrong direction on my Christian walk had my conscience hitting me daily. I knew this was a mistake, but I could not make it through those sink holes filled with water. The rain stopped; the sun came out. The days looked clearer and it seemed I could make this journey again. I turned around and headed back the right way on my Christian walk. Once again, it started smoothly, then the obstacles began to appear, one by one. I expected them, I had done this before, so I continued, not detoured, until I reached those sink holes filled with water, again. I could not swim, so I turned around, again.

Once again, heading the wrong way, I saw the rain stop and the sun come out. Again, I turned around and continued my Christian walk, until I came to those sink holes filled with water. I cannot remember how many times I turned back, until I realized that I had wasted and ruined too much of my life turning back from GOD. Determined, I continued back on my Christian walk, ready for those sink holes filled with water. Cautiously I stepped into those holes and realized that I could stand and walk through them. How much time had I wasted running away from these sink holes filled with water?

I reached the point in my Christian walk where I could dance over the speed bumps and mountains and walk through those sink holes filled with water. I was doing fine and the rain did not detour me, until I found myself up to my neck in water, walking through one of those sink holes. The sink holes were getting deeper. I was not turning back. *I cannot swim*, I thought. *How will I overcome this obstacle?*

At about this point in my walk with CHRIST, I was faced with an obstacle that I felt I could not overcome. *Does GOD want me to fail?* I wondered. *I will not turn back. But I cannot swim. How will I make it across?* Determined to please my FATHER, I put my trust in HIM as I got in those sink holes and began to float. I found that I was moving in circles, getting nowhere, so, I kicked my legs and moved my arms while I floated. I was swimming. Through my faith in GOD, I taught myself to swim across the troubling waters in my life.

Learning to swim made every obstacle easier to overcome. The fear of what was ahead no longer burdened me. I bounced over the speed bumps and mountains, and swam across those sink holes filled with water. Then, the lights went out. That is when I realized that the more obstacles I conquered, the more obstacles I would face. I will not turn back. I will trust, in the darkest hours, in my FATHER.

LORD, guide me.

Day 31

"When JESUS heard it, HE saith unto them,
'They that are whole have no need of the physician,
but they that are sick: I came not to call the righteous,
but sinners to repentance.'"

Mark 2:17

Never leave a man behind!

Some of us, who call ourselves believers, are so quick to judge and separate ourselves from non-believers. If we take all the non-believers and leave them behind, then we the believers go in another direction, who will help to bring the non-believers to CHRIST? What would then become our goal as believers? What will we work toward?

When we decide that our belief in GOD makes us better than those who are "sinful," we have already become the problem. We have failed in our duties as believers to help the fallen soldier. If you see your brother doing something wrong, and the love of CHRIST in you hurts to see them failing, see it as an opportunity to help lift them up, not to bring them down. Some of us would sooner push them off the cliff than to help them off the ledge. We just want to point out everyone's faults and put it on display. That does not make us look very good. I think it is a truly ugly characteristic for a person of GOD to have. Our walk with CHRIST should come from our heart and not our head. We should not be CHRIST-like when it warrants applause, and then back-stabbing underneath it all. Do you think GOD is not watching?

When we truly form a relationship with GOD, it will show in our hearts first. GOD lives in our hearts, and from there, HE pumps HIS life throughout the rest of our existence. Our hearts full of GOD will not allow us to back-bite, lie, cheat, discourage, criticize, and gossip about our backslidden brothers and sisters in CHRIST. Do you really think there will be people in the New Jerusalem sitting and laughing at their enemies who are burning in hell? I pray to GOD that the New Jerusalem will not have such heartless people. The New Jerusalem is going to be filled with beautiful people, with genuine hearts, who wished that everyone made it in. There will not be a dry eye there, because all of the compassionate, GOD-fearing and loving people will be there, broken in two over someone burning in hell. Think about that. If your heart is not full of love, if you have evil intentions for others, if you delight in other people's suffering, if you enjoy gossiping about someone's mistakes rather than helping them get back up, the New Jerusalem will not be a place for you. Call me judgmental, but, those are characteristics of Satan, and I doubt anything less than the pure in heart will make it past the pearly gates. This is why we are told to be CHRIST-like. JESUS CHRIST is not that kind of PERSON! If GOD can see hope in those who seem hopeless, why can't we? We, too, were once considered hopeless; as a matter of fact, to some, we still are.

Let me remind you of the story of Jonah, found in Jonah chapters 1–4. The evil of Nineveh had come to the LORD's attention, and HE was angry with them. The LORD sent Jonah to warn Nineveh that in 40 days HE would destroy the city. Jonah tried to avoid the task of warning Ninevah, and in the end he was caught in a terrible storm, thrown overboard in the middle of the ocean, and swallowed by a whale, whose belly he occupied for three days and three nights. When Jonah came to realize that he could not escape the assignment of GOD, he relented and followed the instructions of GOD to warn Ninevah. Hearing that the wrath of GOD was upon his city, the King of Ninevah put the entire city on a fast, man and beast, and prayed that GOD would forgive them and change HIS mind about destroying the city. GOD heard their prayers and did not destroy the city.

> *"But it displeased Jonah exceedingly, and he was very angry. And he prayed unto the LORD, and said, 'I pray thee, O LORD, was not this my saying, when I was yet in my country? Therefore I fled before unto Tarshish: for I knew that THOU art a gracious GOD, and merciful, slow to anger, and of great kindness, and repentest thee of the evil. Therefore now, O LORD, take, I beseech THEE, my life from me; for it is better for me to die than to live.'" (Jonah 4:1-3)*

Jonah's anger was not like some of ours who would have wished that GOD destroyed the city. Jonah was angry because he knew that GOD would forgive them and felt that the trip to Ninevah was unnecessary.

What is really going on in our hearts? Are we content to let others burn in hell? Are we happy about the downfall of our brothers and sisters? Our hearts should not be willing to let someone suffer. When the LORD returns, we should want to see everyone going up there. I am not trying to fill hell. I don't even want my enemies down there, because Satan is not my friend, he is my greatest enemy. Just the fact that he is not a friend of any should help us to bind together in a stronger force to fight against this common enemy. Let the love of CHRIST shine through us. Let us love one another, let us not leave a man behind. Let us help each other to get to heaven.

Remember, as believers, we are all brothers and sisters. That person we see falling was created by GOD and is loved by GOD. GOD is not sitting in heaven enjoying the way we tear each other down. I believe, GOD, in all HIS love and compassion, rejoices when HE sees us pulling each other up. This is why CHRIST asks, how can we love GOD whom we have never seen, and not love our brother who we see all the time? If we love GOD, we want to make sure not to leave a man behind. GOD is going to be very heartbroken on Judgment Day. HIS heart will break for every soul who did not make it in. I don't know about anyone else, but after all this trouble on Earth, I really want to sit in front of a happy GOD! Heaven is not a competition, there is enough room for everyone.

Do you know of someone who people have just been content to let slip away? Do you know a person who is living a lifestyle contrary to the will of the FATHER, yet, instead of helping them, everyone has just found comfort in talking about them? How can you now begin to nurture your brother or sister in a more positive way, helping them to get closer to the FATHER, without being terribly offensive?

_____
_____
_____
_____
_____
_____
_____
_____
_____
_____
_____
_____

Day 32

*"To ME belongeth vengeance, and recompence;
their foot shall slide in due time:
for the day of their calamity is at hand,
and the things that shall come upon them make haste."*

Deuteronomy 32:35

"Vengeance is MINE," saith the LORD!

If there is one lesson I would like to teach the world, it is this: When you put your faith in GOD, you need not worry about those who thrive on bringing you pain. GOD said HE will repay, and HE does. I know what it's like to stew in discomfort. Every day I wonder when GOD will justify me. There were times when I just fumed. For years I held things in, and I just could not let go of them. One of the things I could never seem to get past was being lied about. People will tell you to just get over it. However, the Bible tells us that even GOD hates a lying tongue, so I felt I was right in despising a liar.

I don't know why I continue to hold things in. I have seen GOD deal my enemies their just rewards. I'll tell you the secret, just give it to GOD and leave it. For you, being lied about may not be more painful than something else you are battling with when it comes to your enemies, but for me, this is my crutch. This is the one thing that hurts me more than anything else. I would sooner forgive those who do me some physical harm. But lie on me, especially in my face? I couldn't forgive it, I just couldn't, and never would I forget. I have told lies in my life. I'm sure many of us have told a few lies, especially in our childhood when the belt was out. I would lie JESUS right off the cross to get out of a beating. But we were children then. There are people who tell those creative lies to make themselves seem a bit more appealing. These lies, although just as sinful, did not bother me as much as that grown adult who would lie to you with a straight face, in your face. Those are the ones who got me down on my knees, because I believed someone like that could do anything to you.

I am sure the LORD knew how much it burned inside of me, and because of this, HE was even more proud of me, for letting it burn and not retaliating. When GOD told us not to take revenge on our enemies, HE knew that HE would be best to handle it. When we take revenge, we open new, unwanted doors to more displeasure in our lives. We need to learn to just be still, pray, and make sure that our actions are not satisfying to the enemy. We would be shocked to know what Satan would do just to get us to do the wrong thing. GOD knows that we are human, and that we have emotions. HE knows that the hurtful things we go through in life may entice us to react. Our anger is not a sin, but what we do in our anger may be . . .

> *"Be ye angry, and sin not: let not the sun go down upon your wrath: Neither give place to the devil." (Ephesians 4:26-27)*

I have found, based on my first-hand experience, when your enemies wrong you and you take revenge, GOD will punish you both. But when they wrong you, and you are still and pray, you can wait and watch; GOD will repay their wrong doing. There is a difference with the person who wrongs you, and feels sorry for what they have done. They will very likely come to you and ask forgiveness and even attempt to right their wrong. In this, we have to be prepared to forgive.

But then there are those who really try us, those unrepentant and vindictive humans who forever antagonize us, those humans who seem not to even believe in GOD, those humans who see no wrong in what they have done, those humans! Those humans are hard to love, but still we are commanded to love them, and though they may make no apologies, still, we must forgive.

In this very light, I also want to say, sometimes we have wronged people and then we come to GOD and ask forgiveness, yet, we do not apologize for the pain we have caused each other. What about the harm that we have done? The job we have cost someone, the relationships we have ruined, the pain we have planted in someone's heart that may never go away?

I was bullied throughout Primary School. I was the girl you would beat up to earn your friendship with the "in" crowd. I never fought back. Even the people who were supposed to be my friends would just push me around just for kicks. Children can be so cruel. Back in the fourth grade a new girl joined our class. She didn't have any friends. I cannot remember quite how it started but I found myself picking on her one day when there were only four of us in the classroom. I was being encouraged by the other two, who would usually bully me around. It made me feel good to have them seemingly on my side. The poor girl started to cry, and I took the dirty mop and wiped her face with it. My two classmates laughed and I felt good to be the one not being bullied for a change. I had forgotten all about that incident until about 18 years later, when I was feeling all depressed about how people have treated me in my life. GOD reminded me that I was not always the victim. I searched long and hard for that young lady. I found her about two years ago and apologized. She barely remembered the incident. I envy people who can have unpleasant experiences and forget all about them. However, whether she remembered or not, I remembered that there was at least one time when I had done some wrong to someone who did not deserve it.

Let us be reminded as we go through this life, that we are not always the victim. Let us focus on the hurt we have caused others. While we may be waiting for GOD to take HIS revenge on someone else, is there someone waiting for GOD to take revenge on us? This is something to think about. This sword cuts both ways, and it is a dreadful thing to fall into the hands of the living GOD. Change ... let it begin with us. Let us be the change we hope to see in others, lest we find ourselves on the receiving end of GOD's vengeance.

Is there someone in your life that you are waiting for the FATHER to rain HIS vengeance on? Is there possibly someone waiting for the FATHER to rain HIS vengeance on you? If the person who offended you came and asked forgiveness, are you prepared to forgive? Have you asked forgiveness of those you have offended? What would you prefer, peace with your enemy or to see them punished? CHRIST hung on a cross asking GOD to forgive those who put HIM there. Have your enemies done something so unforgivable to you? Are you prepared to accept the apology that was never issued?

_____

_____

_____

_____

_____

_____

_____

_____

Day 33

"When JESUS understood it, HE said unto them, 'Why trouble ye the woman? For she hath wrought a good work upon ME. For ye have the poor always with you; but ME ye have not always. For in that she hath poured this ointment on MY body, she did it for MY burial. Verily I say unto you, Wheresoever this gospel shall be preached in the whole world, there shall also this, that this woman hath done be told for a memorial of her.'"

Matthew 26:10-13

(see Matthew 26:6-13 for the story of the Anointing at Bethany)

Is your life Gospel worthy?

No matter what your translation preference is, the Bible is universal. The Bible exists because people we have never met took the time to document some miraculous events surrounding GOD, which they felt would be beneficial in encouraging believers and converting non-believers. The Bible is the most popular book in the world, and although there are places where you can get it absolutely free, I am almost certain it is the most sold book to date. The Bible has been translated into many languages, with its contents being the most popular among scholars. Humans, young and old, believers and non-believers can recite the Scriptures and know the books, characters, and events by heart. It is safe to say, there has never been anyone walking the face of the Earth, who is more popular than the outstanding characters in the Bible.

Like any good book, the Bible has its heroes and its villains. Some of us have never taken the time to read the book from beginning to end, so we do not even know the difference. Some of us believe every action in the Bible is the right thing to do, but that is not the case. Some of us live by a Scripture, not knowing what came before that Scripture, to whom it was said, or why. The Bible is also a history book. Every character in it is not a role model for godly living.

There are some characters in the Bible whose name we sing every time we want to encourage someone. Don't we love to talk about Job? Don't we love to talk about Abraham and Noah? Don't we love to talk about David? How we love to talk about Jacob, as he is the father of the twelve tribes of Israel. But did you even know that the victim of the first rape in the Bible was Jacob's daughter, Dinah? Did you know that after her rape, her two brothers, Simeon and Levi, took a sword and slaughtered all the men of Shechem, including her rapist? The story of Dinah can be found in Genesis 34. We love to talk about Lot, but mostly his wife turning into a pillar of salt when fleeing Sodom and Gomorrah. Did you know that Lot's two daughters both had sons by their father? After they left Sodom and Gomorrah, the girls decided that there were no men to marry them and that they should get their father drunk and lay with him to conceive, which they both did. Did you know? The story of Lot and his daughters is found in Genesis 19:30-38. We love to talk about Sodom and Gomorrah, but did you know about the town of Gibeah, which is of the tribe of Benjamin? This town was also filled with sexual perverts, who raped and beat the concubine of a man from the tribe of Levi so terribly that it led to her death. This incident led to a war against the Benjamites, in which every man and beast of Gibeah was killed, except about 600 which escaped. This man from the tribe of Levi, actually took the dead body of his concubine, cut her up in 12 pieces and sent each piece to every tribe of Israel. After learning what had happened to her, they decided to go to war against this town. The story of the Levite's concubine is found in the book of Judges chapters 19 and 20.

What I want to ask you is, if someone decided to write a Bible for the present day, and leave it behind for the next generation, so that they would know that the GOD we serve today, is the same as the GOD of Abraham, Isaac, and Jacob, would you make the pages? If you did make the pages, what would your character be? Would you be someone people would talk about when they wanted to encourage someone else? Or, would you be the villain? Did you know that, although not written on paper, your life is already being viewed? You are already leaving a chapter behind. What will people say about you? This is something for us all to reflect on. The reality is, no matter how much good we do in this world, people will always reflect on the worst part of us.

Going forward, be careful what you are leaving behind, and in the end, make sure your legacy is good in heaven.

Which Bible character can you relate to, and why? Which Bible character would you prefer to be more like and what can you do to imitate them better?

_____
_____
_____
_____
_____
_____
_____
_____
_____
_____
_____
_____
_____

Day 34

*"But without faith it is impossible to please HIM:
for he that cometh to GOD must believe that HE is
and that HE is a rewarder of them
that diligently seek HIM."*

Hebrews 11:6

GOD's silence.

After I was wrongfully terminated from one of my many jobs, I went to war with GOD. How could GOD allow something like this to happen to me? I pray and put my trust in HIM for everything. I didn't understand this at all. Where was the miracle that was supposed to sweep in and rescue me? How could GOD allow my enemies to be victorious over me this way?

After fasting over it and praying, I waited for GOD's plan to be revealed. I got no answers, no signs, nothing from GOD at all. For two years I slipped in and out of depression, coming to terms with the silence of GOD. Have I been holding on to a GOD who does not even care about me? Why would GOD abandon me this way? I would go into my prayer closet, shut the door, light my candle, prepare to pray, and not be able to get a word out. I had been praying every day for so long and nothing happened. Nothing I could say seemed to be getting GOD's attention. *What do I do now?* I wondered. *What do I do when the GOD I have held so firmly to, seems to have left my life? Where do I go from here? What life is there to live without GOD?* I was lost, hurt, and frustrated. I needed GOD and could not find HIM. I had often wondered if GOD was punishing me for some wrong I had done.

A friend asked me to do her a favor. She needed me to make a publication out of some information. After she sent the information, I logged off the Internet to get rid of the distractions, went into my room and got to work. I could hear my phone going off. It was her wondering how far I had gotten and if I had a chance to get it done. I didn't answer. I was just too into what I was doing, which was what she needed me to do. What she really wanted done was to have the information all put into a tri-fold brochure. It was far too lengthy, but, I did it her way and showed her how the information would not fit neatly in a brochure. Then, I did it in a booklet, so she would see the difference. How I wished she would not bother me with text messages while I'm working. It is annoying. In which direction do you want me to invest my time and energy, doing your project or playing text tag with you?

She was understandably anxious, considering that I had asked her to do something for me a few days earlier, which I was paying her to do, and got no answer. No worries, after all, this wasn't between her and me. GOD was watching and wanted to see if I would repay evil for evil, or, if I would do the right thing. Maybe while she texted, she thought I would not complete the task because I did not answer. She may have thought that I was getting even. It's not that I didn't want to answer. While she may have thought I was ignoring her, I was doing what she needed, and didn't feel the need to give her a step-by-step update of my progress. When it was done, she would have it and be satisfied.

In everything there is a lesson, if we just sit still and be silent long enough to understand. Most times, it calls for what most of us don't have, patience. I have asked GOD for some challenging things. Of course, nothing is too hard for HIM, but there are things we know we should not have because it can sometimes become a distraction from our relationship with CHRIST. Some of us are so bold.

Not only do we ask for these things, we give GOD a time frame. "LORD, I want to open a bar and I need it open by the end of the month." Sometimes you even get it. It's a great wonder how much GOD loves us, how many allowances HE makes for our comfort.

We realize and appreciate by now, that GOD does not move according to our timetable. How many times have we prayed and fasted and cried over something and it felt like we were battling all alone, like GOD had left us? We always need a "right now" answer. We want a quick fix. We forget that GOD is in control and that HE has mapped out the solution to the problem before you even experienced it. We forget that GOD knows what we need and when we will need it. We forget that GOD is GOD. When HE's silent, HE is working. Trust in that. Trust that HE loves you enough to save you from the distress. Trust that HE knows how much of it we can take and just when to step in. GOD is the ultimate Super Hero. When HE constructs a solution to your problem, HE corrects from the foundation to the roof top. GOD does not patch, he repairs.

True faith is trusting in GOD even when it seems HE is not there; *especially* when it seems HE is not there. When you find yourself battling GOD's silence, feeling abandoned, remember, when CHRIST cried out to GOD from the cross, asking why HE had forsaken HIM, GOD did not answer.

Day 35

"And Jabez called on the GOD of Israel, saying,
'Oh that THOU wouldest bless me indeed,
and enlarge my coast, and that THINE hand
might be with me, and that THOU wouldest
keep me from evil, that it may not grieve me!'
And GOD granted him that which he requested."

1 Chronicles 4:10

LORD, please enlarge my territory!

If my life has no other meaning in this world I pray that it has meant something to GOD. I pray that in the end, I can reflect on something positive, knowing that I have given great dedication to the service of GOD. What I do may not be found significant to others, but if I could reach just one person, if I can convince some non-believer of the greatness of GOD, then my work is not in vain. I have been praying for a while that GOD will enlarge my territory, not in riches, but in audience. I would like to be able to reach more people. But, it is true what JESUS said in the book of Matthew:

> "And they were offended in HIM. But JESUS said unto them, 'A prophet is not without honour, save in his own country, and in his own house.'" (Matthew 13:57)

Friends and family are often the very last to support us in these endeavors. Even CHRIST suffered the same. Something would come out of your mouth and not be supported, but they would hear it from a stranger and celebrate it. Such is the same for that stranger whom they celebrate. There are people familiar to them who would not take them as seriously as they take another, whom they do not know. This is a cycle.

Now, I used the Scripture Matthew 13:57, but I am no prophet. I just share what I have learned and experienced in my life. I am praying now that I can share those experiences with more people, to tell them about GOD. However, I have learned that my FATHER would not consider me worthy of a greater audience if I am not willing to speak of HIM to the little audience I may have. We have to show ourselves worthy of the "more" or the "enlargement" we are asking for, by the gratitude we display in the "little."

Some years ago a friend of mine really wanted a Jeep. She and I went down by the car lot, where I stood on the side lines as she prayed, sang, and danced around the brand new Jeep she believed GOD would bless her with, even though she did not have the first penny. She didn't even have a job. This was many years ago, so I cannot quite remember how long it was before her husband purchased an old Maxima for her. It was running fine and just needed to be licensed. Even further back, someone had given her a car. It was a used Neon which she gave them back. That car just needed a battery. The Maxima sat in the front of the yard for what seemed like an eternity, because it was not the Jeep she wanted. Now, my old friend was catching the bus at this point and if it rained her children did not go to school, because there was no transportation.

One day I called to see how she was doing, and she was not doing well. The neighborhood children were playing around the car and had cracked the windshield of the Maxima with a rock. Personally, I thought that may have been the work of the LORD, seeing that the car was not appreciated in the first place.

I always use the example, if you ask the LORD for a bakery, HE will start you off with a loaf of bread. If you cannot show gratitude for a loaf of bread, why should GOD give you anything more? Why do you feel you deserve to have more than the little you are being so ungrateful toward?

When you give it reasonable thought, you will find that it is all for your own good. GOD gives you the "little" to prepare you for the "lot." HE does not want you making the lasting errors when you have the best in your hands. See the little as an opportunity for training. It is no different than a job promotion. You have to excel in your current position before you are found worthy of more responsibility. At least that is the way it is supposed to work.

The prayer of Jabez is well known by so many, especially those of us petitioning the throne for something more than we have. Realize that Jabez being found worthy does not automatically qualify every Christian for the same. Think about the things you are praying to increase. Are you showing appreciation for the little you already have? Have you shown responsibility in caring for the blessings GOD has already granted you, regardless of how small they may seem? What are your intentions for that blessing? What good will this gift bring, and what praise will GOD secure from it? Or, an even better question, what harm may come from the thing you are praying for, and will it bring you closer or take you further from GOD?

As we pray for enlargements in our territory, let us ensure that the increase will not decrease our chances of spending eternal life with our LORD and SAVIOR. HIS withholding of our desires may very well be saving our souls. Also, are we prepared, are we matured, is our foundation in CHRIST strong enough that no increase will distract us from our Christian walk?

Can you think of something that you are praying for an increase in, meanwhile neglecting something that GOD may be using to prepare you for the "more"? Maybe it is a new car, while the old car is mistreated, or a better job, while the old job does not get the best of you. Are you praying for an increase in your finances, but your spending habits are poor toward what you already have? For example, asking the FATHER for $500 to pay off a light bill, but when HE gives you $50 you spend it on other things, instead of putting it on the bill you are trying to pay off. Is there something in the way you may be treating the "little," that may lead the FATHER to withhold the "more?" How can you find new appreciation in the things you have abandoned because they are not exactly what you wanted?

_____

_____

_____

_____

_____

_____

_____

Day 36

"For GOD so loved the world, that HE gave HIS only begotten SON, that whosoever believeth in HIM should not perish, but have everlasting life."

John 3:16

You don't know love like GOD knows love!

If GOD one day told me, "Katrina, you can give ME back one of your organs or parts, and you will not die without it." I would say, LORD, take this heart, and destroy it once and for all. Do not give it to anyone else, because I would not want anyone to know the pain this heart can bring.

I have cried myself to sleep many nights. I have fought spiritually with GOD many times. I've thought of walking away from life a time or two. I wished there was an exit button I could press without killing myself, just in case I wanted to return later—all because of the pain this heart has brought me. My heart, my love, cannot hold a candle to GOD's everlasting and immeasurable love for us.

Do you know what it feels like to really love someone, with everything in you, to have the best intentions for that person, to care for that person like no one else can, to know in your heart that you mean them only good and positive things, then, to have that person you love so much just walk all over you, hurt you, abuse you, mistreat you, and focus on someone or something else? That is a hurt that no medication, no remedy, no words can heal. That is a hurt that only time can repair. But, what if you love that person so much that no amount of time or distance can take the pain away? To feel that hurt over and over and over, and no matter how you try to love them, they just keep hurting you? That is a hurt that hurts eternally. That hurt comes from a love that is eternal, a love you don't know.

Imagine, if you can, being so loved by someone, that no matter what wrong you have done, they cannot stop loving you. Imagine, if you can, being so loved by someone, to whom all of your faults, flaws, and malfunctions are completely insignificant. Can you imagine being so loved by someone that they would revolve the earth around you? Can you imagine a love that never dies, a love without limits just for you? You don't know love.

Can you imagine unjustly hurting someone relentlessly, and when you need them, you run to them, and they just open the door, hold you, and ask no questions, show no spite, point no fingers, relive no errors? Can you imagine such a love? Can you imagine someone loving you so much that they would never sleep, just so they can watch over and keep you safe? You don't know love.

Now, imagine, if you can, this love coming from the most powerful BEING the world has ever known. Imagine, if you can, the very BEING that created the world, placed every star in the sky, created humanity and every good thing under the sun. Just imagine, if you can, GOD, in all HIS greatness, loving someone as insignificant as you and I.

When we get into relationships of any kind, family, friends, lovers, and we give our all, and they mistreat us and take us for granted, we hurt. But I would choose to feel that pain eternally, than to feel GOD's pain for just a minute. I cannot imagine the heart that hurts in GOD, the heart that hurts from our rejection.

GOD, who has the presidency of the Earth itself, running this all and securing everything in it, loves you, adores you, cares for you, celebrates you. Is that a love you want to walk all over? Is that a love you want to throw away? Is that a love you want to take for granted? You don't know love, you will never know love, you will never see love, you will never feel love, you will never hear of love like GOD's love. We have a privilege, but how we take it for granted.

In the same way that GOD knows love, GOD knows hurt. Yes, we bring the most powerful BEING down to HIS knees. We bring tears to the eyes of GOD with all our hurt and rejection, yet, HE keeps HIS arms open to accept us every time, knowing we will once again bring HIM pain. What a love!

For GOD so loved us all, that HE gave HIS only SON to die for us, and yet, we have preferred to love this world, and the things that are not of GOD. GOD's heart is hurting, not just for one or two of us, but for this entire world. What a pain that must be, a pain I pray I would never know. GOD's entire existence is for us, to love us, to care for us, to provide for us. We are what GOD lives for, yet, we take HIM for granted. We have rejected the biggest heart this world can hold, and it hurts GOD. The oceans exist, because GOD's tears are many. I do not want to imagine the pain GOD must feel.

Are we willing to stop? Are we ready to wipe the tears from the face of our CREATOR, and to give back the love HE has designed us to display? What a pain that must be. To give someone a heart to love you, and they take that heart and love someone or something that can never love them like they were meant to be loved. I do not want to imagine the pain GOD endures. The pain we suffer cannot be compared. And what's more, when we are in pain, we go to GOD for comfort, even though we have given HIM more pain than we could ever overcome. Who comforts GOD when the pain gets too much? You will never know hurt like GOD knows hurt. You don't know love like GOD knows love.

I am certain that there has been at least one person in your life who has left you hurt. Take a minute to reflect on that pain. What did they do that hurt you so bad? Now, is there something you may have done or may still be doing that leaves GOD hurt? Maybe there is something standing in the way of your relationship with the FATHER, but you love it too much to let it go. Can you think of something that you can eliminate from your life that would finally put a smile on the face of the FATHER? How can you work toward making your relationship with GOD a better one, a happier one, one more pleasing to HIM?

_____

_____

_____

_____

_____

_____

_____

_____

Day 37

"Now the just shall live by faith: but if any man draw back, MY soul shall have no pleasure in him."

Hebrews 10:38

Where GOD works, Satan plays!

Anyone who has ever put a need before GOD has noticed at least one thing—the more you pray for something, the further away it seems to get.

There was a time when I was afraid to pray for something I really wanted. I thought it would mean losing it. Every time I asked the LORD for something, it appeared that it became the most unreachable thing. When I was younger and inexperienced about life, I used to think GOD hated me so much that HE took the things away when HE knew I liked them. I have had moments in my life where I woke up thanking GOD for something I had, and by nightfall, it was gone, because something angered me and I either gave it away or destroyed it. We just have to give Satan his credit. He sure is an excellent manipulator. Satan, if you allow him, can make you think something you can reach out and grab is actually untouchable, like those blessings GOD is preparing for you.

I did not have a car for about a year. My 1998 Dodge Neon had quit working the minute I brought it from Abaco to Nassau. "Gloria", I called her, was an Abaco girl and didn't take kindly to the busy Nassau highways, so she just gave up on me. Public transportation was limited in my area, so getting around got very hectic. I would have to walk about 25 minutes from the bus stop to my door. I didn't mind that much, except I had started soap making as a hobby, and most times I would be making that long walk with heavy boxes of soap supplies. I would not even complain about how many times I got wet in the rain, making that walk with soap supplies. But I will admit that it was enough to frustrate me.

I am not one to pray for material things but I could not seem to save a dollar to save my life. I needed GOD to help me. I prayed that GOD would help me with transportation. Making only $325.00 a week, I was looking for something I could afford quickly. I saw it as a huge blessing when I found a mechanic willing to sell an old Toyota Windom for $500.00. I paid for it as quickly as I could, even though it didn't start when I checked it. The mechanic's promise to fix it in record time was enough for me to hold on to hope. Weeks went by with my money already paid and he had not fixed the Windom. He and I got in to it and I told him he needed to fix it or give me my money back. I am so often taken advantage of that I foresaw that this was going to leave me very hurt. I prayed about it, "LORD, please let all end well with this."

The bus usually runs across my door until 9:30 a.m. in the morning, so even though my day did not start until about 12:00 noon, I hopped on that bus to avoid the twenty-five minute walk I still had to take on the way back home. This morning I felt lazy about getting ready early, so opted to take the half hour walk to the other bus. I am on the bus and of the thousands of cars in New Providence, which car should be driving parallel to the bus I am sitting on, the very one I paid for. The mechanic had resold my car and pocketed my money. I gave him a call and it took about three months to get most of my money back.

The Windom was not the story I wanted to focus on, but it leads up to it. After the Windom frustration, I called a friend of mine who owns a car rental place and asked if he had any cars I could pay on while he kept it. I figured, although more affordable, it may be better to avoid the three figure car sales. He had a 2005 Buick Century he wanted $2,500.00 for. I talked him down to $2,000.00. What I really wanted was a van or a Jeep, something a little higher off the ground. However, I was just too frustrated with not having transportation to be fussy. Besides, the 2003 Dodge Caravan he had was $3,000.00. I would never be able to afford that. Christmas was coming and I wanted something I could pay off before the holidays, especially since he kept the car until I paid for it in full. The Buick was more in my budget, and having $800.00 in hand already, it took just about a month to pay it off. I did not feel very comfortable in that car. I felt so ungrateful. For all the praying I was doing, my appreciation for finally having a car was barely there.

One day I was driving around with a friend of mine and she mentioned that she wanted a car. I told her I paid $2,000 for it and if she could find that, she could have my blessed Buick. She did just that and purchased my car about a week later, only the third week of my having it. I took that money straight to my friend at the car rental place and told him I would begin paying on the Dodge Caravan, the one I thought I could never afford. Prayer is better than money. In about two months, I had not only paid the $3,000 he wanted for the Caravan, I had also paid $625.00 to have it painted and looking as nice as my Buick Century did. Through prayer and great sacrifice, I had landed the transportation I really wanted. My Caravan was looking good, working fine and fully paid for. I should have been so excited.

Someone had wired the alarm system into the horn of "Morning Gloria," the name I gave my 2003 Dodge Caravan. Anything that brushed past me would set this long, annoying horn off. It was humiliating. It was so humiliating that I was intimidated every time I sat behind the wheel of my blessed Caravan. I would have places to go and things to do and not move because I was uncomfortable in the blessing that GOD had given me. I became so frustrated with this horn situation that I set out to sell "Morning Gloria," my gift from GOD. I no longer wanted the transportation I had always wanted. I would look at "Morning Gloria" and feel nothing but disappointment.

I had been saving to have "Morning Gloria" licensed and insured in my name. She was still under the registration of the previous owner. The night before I was to go and have the licensing and insuring done, I found myself faced with a decision. I had to decide whether I was going to put "Morning Gloria" in the papers for sale, or, if I was going to license and insure my blessing from my FATHER, the blessing I wanted to give up. Around 6:20 a.m. in the morning, I was passing my Caravan on the way from jogging. I felt uneasy about having to drive her today. I prayed, "LORD, please forgive me for being ungrateful. I appreciate my blessing of transportation, but right now I don't feel comfortable in the ride. LORD, please, give me peace in my blessed van."

The time came for me to go on the road. I waited until after the morning rush to avoid most traffic. I took the horn fuse out of "Morning Gloria" so the horn would not annoy me or anyone else. Yet, I was still nervous and intimidated in her. I had to go to my friend's to get the Bill of Sale, which he would give me only upon returning his license plates. I asked someone to go with me so they could sign on the witness line, but the truth was I did not want to be alone in my Caravan. I had exactly $500.00. It would cost about $265.00 for the cheapest insurance I could find and I estimated about $210.00 to license "Morning Gloria." I need not say that by this time my mind was made up not to sell her, well, not today anyway. My friend got in the car with me and we went and got the Bill of Sale, but not before stopping to the inspecting company to have the Caravan approved for insurance. The inspecting company said my Caravan was not old enough for inspection and I didn't need to be there, although instructed by the insurance company. Before I could go to the insurance company, my friend decided that she could not stay with me so I had to drop her off. Now, once again, I'm alone and intimidated in "Morning Gloria."

When I walked into the insurance company and told them that I was told my Caravan was not old enough to warrant an inspection, they told me they got another story from the inspecting company. That was enough for me to tell them I'll just go with another insurance company. Going with another company meant I would have to wait until the next week to insure and license because the next affordable price was $360.00 for insurance. That was about $70.00 more than I could afford. Discouraged now, driving through the heart of town with $500.00 in my purse, I stopped at one of those online casinos. I don't know why I went there, I had not gambled in forever and never get any impulses. I just didn't want to go home, I guess. Or maybe I just needed a quick break from the discomfort I was feeling in "Morning Gloria." I took $100.00 out of the $500.00 in my purse, and within 20 minutes, I had won $400.00. You may find it strange that I thanked GOD for that win, but somehow I didn't think Satan had set out to supply my needs. I took the $400.00 and headed to the nearest insurance company. Now, I could afford insurance with any company I wished.

After I settled in at the second insurance company and everything looked like it was about to go smoothly, they realized that my inspection document was not the original, but a copy. I would have to drive, in traffic, through some busy areas to get that original document and return to the insurance company. Instead, I opted for another insurance company that was closer to where I needed to get the document from. I was back and forth on the road for about four hours in "Morning Gloria" by the time she was licensed and insured. Guess what? I had been doing so much driving, mostly frustrated about the insurance turn-around, that the horn situation slipped my mind and somewhere in the midst of it, I got so comfortable in my blessed Caravan that I spent another two hours just driving around, finally enjoying my blessing, before heading home.

What we don't realize is just how much faith Satan has. Satan has more faith in GOD than any human being could ever muster. When we get down on our knees and begin to pray to GOD, Satan does not wait. He runs right to GOD's workshop and attempts to sabotage the equipment. That equipment usually is our mind. Satan cannot take anything from you. Satan cannot stop you from getting your blessing. What he can do is manipulate your thinking, causing you to walk away from, or give up the blessing GOD has lined up for you.

When GOD begins to work, Satan starts to play. But Satan cannot play with GOD. Satan plays with our minds. He plants those seeds of doubt that begin to make us believe that GOD is not working. When that doubt kicks in, we walk away, we cease to pray. We give up! Satan wins!

Don't give up. When you feel Satan playing in your head, you must persist, keep praying, believe until it happens, or until GOD makes it clear that HE has something better for you. Not everything we want is best for us. Sometimes GOD keeps those things away, through love. Only through praying and a relationship with GOD will we come to know the difference between what GOD withholds and what Satan trifles with.

As for the blessings that GOD has already put in our hands, like my "Morning Gloria," Satan cannot take them out of our hands. He can only frustrate us enough to let them go. Just as my FATHER was faithful to bring me the comfort I needed to appreciate my blessing, I am confident, that with prayer and faith in GOD, you will gain the strength you need to overcome any intimidation Satan may send your way, hoping that he can get you to let go of your blessings. With this we need discernment. Sometimes we think those doubts in our minds, which seem rational, are of GOD. This confusion can cause us to let go of the very things we have prayed that GOD would give us. Here is where we pray and put our trust in our FATHER. A personal relationship with GOD and studying of HIS Word is so vital in our Christian walk.

Continue to trust in the LORD and lean not unto your own understanding, lest you lose your way, your blessing, or your very salvation.

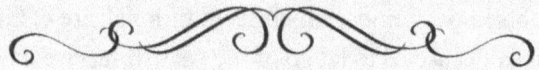

I'm sure we all have had a "Morning Gloria" situation, a blessing that we were prepared to walk away from, just because something about it did not seem right, minor imperfections. Have you ever prayed for something, got it, and then walked away from it because it wasn't what you thought it would be? Can you think of at least one situation where Satan may have attempted to get you to walk away from something wonderful the FATHER had given you? Satan has led me to quit over 30 good jobs since leaving High School, all because I thought I wasn't worthy to stand my ground. I always give my blessings away. Correction, I used to give them away. Is there something in your life right now that you have always wanted, now you have the opportunity to get it, or you may even have it, but you are unsure about holding on to it? Are your reasons for walking away from your blessing rational, or are they as silly as giving up an entire Caravan because of a horn alarm?

_____

_____

_____

_____

_____

Day 38

"Be sober, be vigilant;
because your adversary the devil,
as a roaring lion, walketh about,
seeking whom he may devour."

1 Peter 5:8

Know your enemy!

Since Satan's eviction from heaven, his anger has led him to devote his time to collecting the souls of mankind. This evil genius has found many ways to win human souls, with deception being the cleverest of them all.

Deception has allowed Satan to inhabit our lives and our souls because, refusing to read and know the truth, we fall prey to what we THINK is right. Satan, in his great and undetected wisdom, has convinced a man that it is the right thing to have sex with his own children. Satan, in his great and undetected wisdom, has convinced countless mothers that their children are evil, and that they would be better off dead, leading mothers to murder their own children. Satan, in his great and undetected wisdom, has convinced humans to lie so deeply about each other, that it has caused others their families, their jobs, and even their freedom and very life. Satan, in his great and undetected wisdom, has convinced children to kill their own parents, grandparents, and even their own siblings. Clever is he, for after he has made them murderers, most of them he gains with suicide, ending their lives in the midst of their great sins, securing their souls in hell. Satan, in his great and undetected wisdom, has convinced too many that it is now fine to have sex before marriage. Satan, in his great and undetected wisdom, has convinced men and women, that if their heart feels love for that person they are having that extra marital affair with, then it is meant to be. Satan, in his great and undetected wisdom, has made his legacy the destruction of the family, knowing that where there is no union, fornication and adultery are very likely to exist. Satan, in his great and undetected wisdom, has manipulated others into thinking that the very children of GOD are evil and should be slaughtered for the sake of the kingdom. Satan in his great and undetected wisdom, has confused many into thinking they are safe in the arms of GOD, when the very traditions their church is built on defy the laws of the LORD. This is one of Satan's best tricks to date.

Satan, the master of lies, deception, murder, abuse, suicide, and all things impure, sits in the dark corners and watches with laughter, as his deceptions take root in our lives, knowing that he not only got us to do something abominable, but, he has won us over completely, because we don't want to hear about GOD. Satan takes away all the hope we have in this life, drains us of our joy, cripples us from walking to our blessing, curses our future with his clever disguises, and in the end, he has nothing to offer his followers but a life of torment and eternal damnation.

Satan, in his great and undetected wisdom, has convinced mankind that he is not real, he is not manipulating them, and that it is not worth it to hear about GOD. If you have chosen not to get to know our LORD and SAVIOR, for your sake, I hope you know your enemy, because he knows you.

Day 39

"For the LORD HIMSELF shall descend from heaven with a shout, with the voice of the archangel, and with the trump of GOD: and the dead in CHRIST shall rise first: Then we which are alive and remain shall be caught up together with them in the clouds, to meet the LORD in the air: and so shall we ever be with the LORD. Wherefore comfort one another with these words."

1 Thessalonians 4:16-18

A vision of the second coming!

It was late evening and I had just settled down to rest. Then suddenly, the sound of the trumpet cut like a razor blade through the souls of the unprepared. Silence slaughtered the nature of things, as the hearts of Christians beat more rapidly in great anticipation of the LORD's coming. I saw the confused expression upon the faces of sinners. This was a sound they knew nothing of. Unfortunately, to their dismay, the second coming was no secret rapture.

> "Behold, HE cometh with clouds; and every eye shall see HIM, and they also which pierced HIM: and all kindreds of the earth shall wail because of HIM. Even so, Amen." (Revelation 1:7)

I watched men scurry in a chaotic dance, a foolish attempt to avoid this rapture, which was to them, a nightmare. Nothing like this had been seen before, nor would it be seen again. In great numbers, men fell to the ground as their hearts gave out inside them. The fear of this day, which some thought would never come, was too much for many to bear.

> *"And the heaven departed as a scroll when it is rolled together; and every mountain and island were moved out of their places. And the kings of the earth, and the great men, and the rich men, and the chief captains, and the mighty men, and every bondman, and every free man, hid themselves in the dens and in the rocks of the mountains; and said to the mountains and rocks, 'Fall on us, and hide us from the face of HIM that sitteth on the throne, and from the wrath of the LAMB: For the great day of HIS wrath is come; and who shall be able to stand?'" (Revelation 6:14-17)*

If I had not known my LORD, this day, for me, would be a horrific devastation. I stood, almost fearful, watching the rocks and mountains roll away unassisted, exposing those struck with fear from the reality of the SAVIOR they had rejected. Mercy! They found out, too late, that they were wrong. There truly was a GOD and HE was about to be revealed.

Suddenly, like a flash of lightning frozen in time, a bright light cleaned up the dimness of this passing day. Then, my eyes beheld the glory. I saw my SAVIOR descending in the clouds of thousands of angels, with HIS arms outstretched and tears streaming down HIS face. HIS long white robe danced in the wind I myself could not feel. HE was perfect.

The ground shock beneath me, opening what seemed like random places in the earth. That's when it happened. Just like the Scriptures said it would. The saints, who had passed away, rose from their slumber. Oh to see the joy on their faces. The praises of the children of GOD drowned out the screams of terror, which rung relentlessly from those who had chosen to forget our LORD and SAVIOR. My heart ached for them. I saw mothers and fathers trying to hold on to their children. The pain was evident on their faces as they watched those little ones run toward the cloud of angels.

GOD was calling HIS children and we knew the sound of our SAVIOR, though HIS lips said not a word.

As a chill ran through my body, I heard my brothers and sisters in CHRIST exclaim with an excitement which told me, that just like mine, their bodies had been changed. Then we were lifted up on the clouds to join our SAVIOR, whose feet never touched the ground.

What a day of mixed emotions, when at last my FATHER I met. Yet the pain of those who would never join us was too much to ignore. Sitting on those clouds with the saints, looking at the angels who all seemed individually important to me, seeing the face of my LORD, I knew it would be a while before we could celebrate our victory. This day would have been better if everyone had made it in.

Just as the earth crumbled, opening a great, dark abyss, my alarm clock rung. This was just a dream. One day, one day soon, this will be either a dream realized or a nightmare lived. Which will it be for you?

Day 40

"I will lift up mine eyes unto the hills, from whence cometh my help. My help cometh from the LORD, which made heaven and earth. HE will not suffer thy foot to be moved: HE that keepeth thee will not slumber. Behold, HE that keepeth Israel shall neither slumber nor sleep. The LORD is thy keeper: the LORD is thy shade upon thy right hand. The sun shall not smite thee by day, nor the moon by night. The LORD shall preserve thee from all evil: HE shall preserve thy soul. The LORD shall preserve thy going out and thy coming in from this time forth, and even for evermore."

Psalm 121

My help cometh from the LORD!

Whenever I tell someone I am fasting for 40 days straight, with absolutely no food, they cannot believe it. The first thing you need to know is a spiritual fast is not about weight loss, even though I am very grateful for the 19 pounds I lost during my fast. The next thing I would like to say is, if your faith in GOD is so weak that you cannot believe that HE will strengthen you to go without food for 40 days, please, do not discourage others.

I don't even know where the time went. My fast went by so quickly. I didn't feel the weight of it. From time to time I missed food, of course. It would not be a sacrifice if I did not give up something I would miss terribly. However, I have been able to see the LORD work in miraculous ways. I truly enjoyed my time with the LORD.

I have learned some things along the way. As I prayed that GOD would show me the flaws in my character and help me to be a better person, HE has done exactly that. I can see the ugly, and I will continue to pray for change. My fast was not without incident. I have had some trying moments that made me think about giving up. But when I realized the goal ahead, and when I remembered how faithful GOD is, and I knew my sacrifice would not be in vain, I pressed on.

I have been fasting for more than 10 years. For every time, GOD has answered. It was not always a "Yes." I did not always get what I wanted, but GOD has found one way or another to let me know why I would not receive what I prayed for. That is enough to be thankful for. Then there are the times, when I got what I prayed for, in such jaw-dropping ways, that I knew only GOD could have done it.

I recommend fasting and praying, because I have proven it, over and over and over again. But to get the full benefit of a fast, I recommend a relationship with CHRIST. Before I call myself a Christian, I would say that I am GOD-fearing. I do what I know to be right, because I fear GOD. I live my life considering GOD is always watching. What others think of me and my walk with GOD is irrelevant, because daily, I seek to please GOD. I make mistakes; I am human. But GOD knows my heart, and that is enough to be thankful for. With the relationship I have with GOD, it makes it easier to cope with my trials, knowing there is a lesson in every struggle. Also, it makes it easier to accept HIS "No," when HE has put one of my desires in the "Rejected" pile. I know and appreciate that GOD will make the best decisions for my life.

I pray that as my fast has ended, I will continue to practice and strive toward good characteristics, staying in a sacred state of mind. Don't we do the best when we are fasting? We don't have to starve to do right. We should always do what is right. That is my prayer, to continue in doing what is right.

As I write this last devotion, I would like to leave you with this. If you want to make a sacrifice for GOD, you must do it knowing that GOD is your strength. You must be able to tune out the voices of the carnal mind. You must be able to stand when everyone thinks you should be falling. GOD can do exceedingly and abundantly above whatever your mind can conceive. However, to save wasted time, make sure that what you are praying for is in accordance with GOD's will. We don't like to say that, but in the end, it is the best solution for our lives.

I hope that the experiences I have shared and the lessons I have learned in my life have been an inspiration to you. I pray that, if nothing else, you have been inspired to journey closer to GOD and to allow HIM to use you for the purpose your life was intended.

I do love my FATHER and wish that everyone could taste the goodness of GOD. Please, I beg you, try HIM. There is something about a relationship with GOD that makes life and all of its struggles more tolerable.

The first fast I put before the FATHER got me a "No." I was terribly hurt because I thought fasting guaranteed me a "Yes." Today, I am grateful for that "No." I realize that fasting brings us closer to the FATHER. We are blessed when HE has made a decision for our lives, despite our cries for something contrary to HIS will. Can you think of something you thought you really wanted, that you can look back now and say, "Thank YOU, FATHER that YOU never gave it to me?" If you are praying about something now, are you strong enough to accept a "No" if the FATHER decides that it is not within HIS plan for your life?

_____

_____

_____

_____

_____

_____

_____

_____

About the Author:

The Katrina Highway

The Katrina Highway is nicely paved. It is the smoothest road you will ever travel. Open your sunroof and let your hair down; it will be the sweetest journey. The well-lit road is lined with healthy palm trees and beautiful, blooming roses. There are no speed bumps, pot holes, traffic lights, or detours. As a matter of fact, you will not run into any traffic at all, because there are not a lot of people in this world who want to take a smooth journey down a beautiful and peaceful highway, that leads to nowhere. I have lived my life on the Katrina Highway.

Since graduating High School in the Bahamas in 1994, I have had over thirty jobs. My first job was at a clothing store. The manager and I were friends gone wrong, and she used her powers to intimidate me. The Supervisor said, "I was told to watch you very closely."

"Watch this," was all I was thinking when I picked up my bag and walked out of the door. I didn't look back and I don't think I cared for a minute what happened behind me.

Next, I landed a job as a Bank Teller. My cash came up short $45 and they took it out of my pay check. The very next day, as they were counting my $5 bills, they found a $50 bill in the bundle. So, I came up $45 over. Because my managers refused to admit to their halfway cash check the previous day, they let my overage go unnoticed. I had already paid for it out of my $170 check. I didn't say a word. I got off from work that day and never went back.

A couple months later, I landed a better job, another bank, just a more reputable one. I was doing well there. Then I was transferred to another branch. My supervisor was newly promoted and had that unprofessional attitude of throwing her weight around. Two weeks into my tenure, she called me into a small room, where we counted cash, closed the door behind us and said, "I don't like the way you say, 'Good Morning!' It isn't loud enough and you ring your bell too loud." Shocked, I stood there watching this woman reprimand me while bouncing from side to side like she was ready to knock me over. "And, unfold your arms when I'm talking to you," she continued. After she made sure I read her loud and clear, we exited the room, I handed in my resignation, went to lunch and never returned. I cannot remember why I quit the job that followed, because by then, I had already set a pattern for my life. I would quit a job just because it was raining.

As I came to realize that I no longer had to endure the unpleasant experiences and people in life, quitting a job became easier every time. Although it was easy to walk away, it took a piece of me, every time. Then, as life would have it, my instability trickled into the other aspects of my existence. I gave up and walked away from friendships, relationships, living spaces, and even the islands I lived on. Since I was 18 years old, I have never fully unpacked a suitcase. I have always been ready to leave at the drop of a dime. I never gave anyone a chance to get to know me. Why should I? I never even knew myself.

I go into everything with my temporary glasses on. I see the end of a thing from the very day I begin it. The day I start a job, I have already begun a countdown to the day I'll be leaving. There will not be any retirement parties for this lady. I have only lasted on three of my thirty-plus jobs long enough to take a vacation. The day I start a new relationship, right away I start wondering how this is going to end. I watch the way he treats me, and in my mind, I already know the day will come when he wants me nowhere around. Fearing the approaching rejection, I pack quickly and move on. Even though they didn't have time to reject me, it took a piece of me, every time.

Frederick Douglass once wisely said, "It is easier to build strong children than to repair broken men." Growing up, no one really ever understood me. I grew up in a very strict household. A child was just a child, and there were no round table meetings to discuss your feelings. Keeping my emotions all bottled in took huge pieces of me, every single time I felt the need to defend myself. Misunderstandings and false accusations went uncorrected. Therefore, I entered my adult life with unresolved issues, many unresolved issues, too many unresolved issues. What adults don't understand is that children grow up, but the wounds don't automatically heal; we don't forget, and with no preparation, we don't just mature the minute we become women, especially if we are treated like children all of our lives, right up to being adults. Misunderstood children grow up to be misunderstood adults. For some of us, suicide becomes a desirable way out. For others, who hold on, GOD brings the comfort and security we have lacked.

It has been hard for me to understand and adjust to life. I entered adulthood, broken, too many missing pieces to feel whole.

When people have tried to reach out to me, I withdrew and never tried to socialize, because I don't know how. Social situations made me terribly uncomfortable, because I was never taught to socialize. I was never invited to be a part. I was dealt a painful blow the day I realized that I was not like other people. I seem to lack common abilities that every mature woman should possess. Facing that reality took many pieces of me, making life even harder for me to handle, so I paved the Katrina Highway.

By the time I was twenty-five, my hatred for myself was a concrete element in my life. My self-esteem could not have possibly been any lower. I can remember going in to my private place to pray, and the words just could not come out. I didn't know what to say to GOD. I was so tired of hurting. I was so tired of hoping. I was so tired of longing for a life that it didn't seem GOD intended me to have. GOD, what do I say to YOU? It is a painful frustration to fight a battle with the LORD. What do I say when what I truly long for is denied me? Yet, I cannot turn away from GOD, because HE is the air I breathe. How do you heal a broken woman?

I didn't want to write about my pain on these pages. I didn't want to tell strangers that the girl who is so quick to run, who looks like she doesn't care about anything, thinks the world of everything, and longs for a reason to stop running. I didn't want the world to know that I am a broken woman, broken from the core of my being.

I didn't want to continue down the Katrina Highway, but it was the only home I knew. It was the only place where I felt accepted, because I was the only one there. Every single time I have packed up my life and headed for that highway, I have longed to hear someone say, "Katrina, don't go." I have never heard those words. I have prayed, with tears and pain in my chest; I have prayed. I have asked my FATHER: "Please mend this broken woman and give her a chance at a future." I was afraid to hope and believe, because my dreams are greater than any reality I have ever known.

I can still remember the day I headed down my lonely highway and found that I was not alone. I heard a voice, but saw no one. The voice said, "Be still, and know that I am GOD." GOD saw me heading back down the Katrina Highway, and HE stopped me. HE told me to get up and look ahead.

"Katrina, what do you see?" I saw nothing down that highway. It was nothing but a long road. Suddenly I realized it was just the ride that felt good, the destination was never considered. For 20 years I had been headed down the same road, the same journey, and not until that moment did I realize that I was traveling to nowhere. Although the Katrina Highway is the only home I knew, my home was not a shelter. My home was just an open road that no one else wanted to travel.

How do you heal a broken woman? You give her to GOD. Only GOD can mend what man has destroyed beyond repair. As my FATHER has laid me on HIS operating table and prepared to mend my brokenness, there are times when I want to get off this table and head down the Katrina Highway. Sometimes, I miss home. I miss home, not because it is a wonderful place, but because it is so comfortably familiar.

I am grateful that GOD has taken the time to mend my brokenness. I feel so unworthy of HIS attention, but now, now I can see the beauty in me. GOD has helped me to see that I don't have to be the person that gives up, that walks away, the person that runs. I now see that I can endure as anyone else has. I can succeed as anyone else has. As for the ugliness I once saw in myself, because of the mistakes of my past, I now embrace the beauty of it all, the beauty that says, "Thank GOD—regret is all I walked away with." Despite their attempts to break me, despite the evil that raped me, despite the mistakes that aimed to destroy me, I still have a future to look forward to.

I don't know what GOD has ahead for me as I have taken this healthier highway in life. I don't know if things will get any better or if there are any miracles in store for me. But I do know that I love the LORD, with all of me. HE allowed me to be broken so that I could appreciate the work HE must do in me, and so that the world will glorify my FATHER, knowing that only GOD could have repaired this broken woman.

I pass by the Katrina Highway every so often, and I have been tempted to drop everything, as I have always done, and drive down that road again. But, the last time I went by, I noticed that GOD had put a sign there that reads, "Katrina Highway. CLOSED PERMANENTLY!" That is how this book finally got finished, the first thing in my life I have ever seen through to the end, because I was unable to run down my highway. GOD is faithful.

HE is the only ONE WHO ever said, "Katrina, don't go!"

Conclusion

Who would have thought that I would become a published author at the age of 41? I have been writing since Primary School. I truly believe, without a doubt, that when we commit to the FATHER, when we put our trust in HIM, when we exercise true faith, believing in HIM, without wavering, in the end, HIS will is done in our lives. The reason the children of Israel were not allowed to leave Egypt was not because Pharaoh did not allow them, it was because the FATHER hardened his heart, so that he would not allow them to leave. The testimony may not have been so strong, the story may not have been so exciting, if Pharaoh had let them out at their first request.

I have known for a long time that my wavering mind and unstable ways were not pleasing to the FATHER. Humans, looking at the outward appearance, viewing the results of my impulsive behavior, wrote me off as one who would never accomplish anything. They never saw me on my knees, nor heard my constant prayers. They didn't know that every time I ran, I prayed that my FATHER would help to settle me. It gave me no pleasure walking away from the many blessings HE had bestowed upon undeserving me. I longed for the day I would change. It happened almost as quick as a flash. One day, I just got tired of running. One day, I lost all desire to pack and uproot my life. However, had it not been for my many bad decisions, the many roads I have traveled, the many places and things I have experienced, the many people I have become acquainted with during my fickle moments, this book would have less than ten pages.

There are things in our lives we don't understand, things we may never understand. But what I do understand is, regardless of our many faults, the FATHER sees our hearts and our good intentions. HE knows our struggles and HE will not ignore the cries of HIS children when we plead for the strength to resist the actions which offend HIM. Who am I, or anyone else to assume that my previous, undesirable pattern in life was not the work of my FATHER, preparing testimonies to share with others?

I do not doubt that my FATHER has a plan for every life HE has created. I do not doubt HIS undying love for us all. But we must not waver in our faith. We must stay focused on HIM. Someone once said to me, "You could never be used in ministry." Gratefully, my FATHER doesn't take instructions from man. If I was thinking at the time they made the comment, I would have reminded them, as I am reminding you, that the Paul we so often quote was on his way to slaughter more saints when he was called to ministry. The FATHER uses whom HE wishes, how HE wishes, where and when HE wishes. We need only be willing to enter into HIS service.

There are experiences I have shared in this book that still minister to me. I am encouraged by my own life story. I have enjoyed writing these devotions, even more, I have enjoyed sharing them. There is a testimony in all of us. I may not see the greatness in an event in my past that someone else may see. GOD knows who needs to hear your story. Do not let your praise die with you. Do not let your testimony go unheard. The experience you share may be the very one that wins a soul.

Be encouraged to do great things for the Kingdom, for you have fans in Heaven, cheering you on.

Healthy Life Press
Books, eBooks, DVDs
Arvada, Colorado

A Small, Independent Christian Publisher with a big mission—to help people live healthier lives physically, emotionally, spiritually, and relationally.

For a downloadable PDF catalog of our resources, and access to free sample excerpts from our books, visit: *www.healthylifepress.com*

1-877-331-2766 | *info@healthylifepress.com*

www.ingramcontent.com/pod-product-compliance
Lightning Source LLC
Chambersburg PA
CBHW070053080526
44586CB00013B/1032